How to Travel
the World
for FREE

I did it, and you can do it, too!

MICHAEL WIGGE

7/12
IWB
1200

2 How to Travel the World for FREE

All images: Michael Wigge

To learn more about the author, visit:
www.michaelwigge.com

Email: info@pichu-productions.com

Edited by Nadya Bondoreff

Layout by Dominik Stahl

ISBN: 3000375422
ISBN-13: 978-3000375422

Version 1.2

The Equipment

About the Book

Is it really possible to travel from Berlin to Antarctica without a single cent in your pocket?

Michael Wigge is on the adventure of a lifetime, where even simple necessities become a challenge. What will he eat? Where will he sleep? How will he get from place to place? Every day, these questions (among others) will occupy his thoughts.

Right from the outset, his journey hits the ground running with action and excitement, from playing hide-and-seek with ticket agents on the train to being put to work on a container ship while crossing the Atlantic Ocean to Canada. And this is just the beginning of his trip!

Who will he meet along the way? And—most importantly—how will he get across North and South America to reach Antarctica, his final destination?

This book is full of surprises; some more pleasant than others. Nevertheless, it's an adventure you won't want to miss!

About the Author

Author and journalist Michael Wigge began his career as an anchor for the German VIVA program *London Calling* in 2002. Since then, the world has been his newsroom and playground, whether he is living with the native Yanomami Indian tribe in the Amazon rain forest, taking the longest recorded donkey ride in the history of music television, or fighting Sumo wrestlers in Japan.

Whether reporting from prison for MTV or entering Buckingham Palace solemnly attired as King Henry VIII, Wigge has always thrown himself into the most unusual of situations.

Michael Wigge's most recent adventure involved traveling throughout 14 different countries with the goal of turning a half-eaten apple into a dream home in Hawaii, using only the bartering system. Prior to this, Wigge's other globetrotting escapade found him journeying from Europe to the Americas to, finally, Antarctica (literally the end of the world) without a penny to his name.

Wigge currently lives in Berlin, Germany, but far prefers to be on the move.

Contents

1/ Even Basic Needs Aren't Free
   (Berlin to Antwerp)   8

2/ All Hands Below Deck
   (Antwerp to Montreal)   20

3/ True North, Land of the Free
   (Montreal to Niagara)   27

4/ Go West, Young Man
   (Cleveland to New Mexico)   39

5/ All-American Gigolo
   (Albuquerque)   54

6/ No Gifts in the Wild West
   (Las Vegas)   61

7/ Everybody Has a Dream
   (Los Angeles)   75

8/ Advanced Pillow Fighting
   (San Francisco)   82

Contents

9/ No Trouble in Paradise
   (Hawaii)   94

10/ On the Run from Dr. Luck
   (Costa Rica to Panama)   116

11/ Katarina's Catamaran
   (Colombia)   126

12/ My Life as a Peruvian
   (Peru to Bolivia)   133

13/ A Kingdom for a Guinea Pig
   (Bolivia)   155

14/ The Madman
   (Chile)   160

15/ Ümit Saves the Day
   (Buenos Aires to Tierra del Fuego)   166

16/ The End of the World
   (Antarctica)   179

1/ Even Basic Needs Aren't Free
(Berlin to Antwerp)

It is the 21st of June, which means it is officially the summer solstice, and the longest day of the year. I can actually feel this all over my body. For more than three hours, I have been standing at a freeway exit trying to continue my journey towards Cologne. Thinking of the 25,000 miles I still have yet to cover, it's hard to imagine that five months from now, I will actually set foot on Antarctica—*the end of the world,* as my friends would say—without having a single penny in my pocket.

It may be the longest day of the year, but it also feels like the hottest day of the year: this, together with the equipment on my back, makes the sweat pour down my overheated body like a nasty waterfall. The sun is laughing at me; the cars that pass by also, somehow, snicker with amusement. I'm hitchhiking with a sign on my back that reads *The End of the World!,* so this could possibly have something to do with it. But none of this bothers me, since my mind is already far, far away in Antarctica.

At some point, what I count as the 2,420th car whooshes past me. You see, I have noted eleven cars driving past me about every minute, bringing me to a total of 2,420 cars in exactly 220 minutes—amazing what the mind can do in the heat. If one is optimistic enough to believe what *Lonely Planet* says about Germany being a hitchhiker-friendly country, then one will likely wait for as long as I have been waiting.

Discouraged and soaked with my own perspiration, my Antarctic visions completely dashed, I am just about to give up and call it a day when a red van pulls up. The driver's side window rolls down and a grumbling voice calls out, "Need a ride?"

Arndt and Marius are returning from a convention of Leftists in Berlin. I now sit in their backseat telling them about my crazy plan of reaching Antarctica without having a solitary cent in my pocket. However, as I talk, I realize that I am in desperate need of relief. After being in the sun all day, one would think that I would actually be dehydrated, not needing to expend excess liquid, but my bladder is calling and Marius is kind enough to make a pit stop in my honor. I run as fast as I can to the public toilet, only to be blocked by a gate with a sign that reads: *50 cents*.

Before starting this trip, I had thought of all the possible scenarios that might require money and how to get around them, but even I have to admit that this is one I didn't take into consideration at all. Something like this should be free anyways, shouldn't it? Desperate, I try charming the toilet attendant—not as easy a task as it may sound. I tell her that I have no money, that this is an emergency, and if she could just find it in her heart to let me pass through just this once, *just this one time*, my appreciation would be boundless.

"Get a job."

Knowing that there is no way to convince her, I instead find a few nice bushes around the corner. When I get back to the van, I tell Arndt and Marius about my little...situation. They are both fired up after the convention and effortlessly compare my problem to that of society's class struggles. "You wouldn't find anything like this in socialism!" rants Marius. He's probably right, actually. Maybe socialism isn't so bad after all.

Finally, we reach the first stop on my trip: Cologne, the city in which I lived and worked for six years. From here, the plan is to travel to Belgium, where a container ship is waiting to take me across to Canada. Since the ship won't set sail for five days, I can make use of this time to visit some old friends. However, I'm not completely without ulterior motives: I'm hoping that by catching up with them, I'll also have a free place to crash for the next few nights.

My friend, Hardy, lives with his girlfriend in a perfectly pleasant garden bungalow near the edge of the city, and when I ring his doorbell, I am greeted warmly and immediately offered a comfy couch to stay on—an offer I swiftly accept. As I tell him about my first day, my stomach demands attention by beginning to audibly growl, but Hardy's refrigerator is as empty as my stomach.

We both start wondering where we can get something to eat at this late hour. Now, luckily, some supermarkets in Cologne are still open in the late evening, which is a simple solution if you have money. However, I'm not traveling with any whatsoever, and don't want to ask too much of Hardy's hospitality, so I have another idea:

Dumpster diving it is, then.

A humble act of foraging that apparently originated in the U.S., dumpster diving is new to Germany, and involves getting—quite literally—down and dirty as you search for food in a supermarket's dumpsters. The food is often perfectly edible, if not good, but is simply no longer sellable either due to its expiration date or its not-entirely-appetizing appearance.

I take the local train downtown, which is free for me but which still requires a ticket. (Like in many German cities, public transportation in Cologne allows students and employed monthly ticket holders to participate in a public rideshare, permitting them to take another person along on their pass free of cost, but only after seven in the evening.) Since most shops in the city are closed by now, it will be the perfect time for my…shopping expedition. I set off for the largest supermarket near the city's park, almost more curious than hungry to see if dumpster diving is possible here in Cologne.

Tiptoeing like a burglar and armed with just a flashlight and some plastic bags, I ease behind the building and stand in front of the gate to the supermarket's courtyard. From here I can see the dumpsters, and, motivated by my growling tummy, I somehow manage to climb over the six-foot tall fence. I flash the light into the first dumpster and I nearly die of terror: the beam lands directly onto the face of a man.

"Hey, wait your turn!" he snaps.

I eventually learn that this man is named Peter, and that he studies social work in Cologne. For years now he has been looking for food in this manner—not because of a shortage of money, but because of his ideological refusal of consumption.

"*Freeganism* comes from the word *free* and means free of cost—much in the same way that veganism and vegan relate," explains Peter as he picks out his culinary treasures. "There are proper Freegan scenes here in Cologne. We meet regularly and cook together." Peter gets by with 200 Euros a month, which mainly is for his insurance costs. He gets his food from dumpsters and lives in a construction trailer.

After filling his backpack, Peter lets me have my way with the dumpster. As I fill my bags with yogurt, sausage, bread, cheese, milk, and even some gummy bears, Peter explains to me that, unlike other countries, dumpster diving is actually illegal in Germany. "Even garbage has an owner in this country," he says, "so legally and technically, what we are engaged in here is good old-fashioned *theft*. A few years ago a woman in Cologne was sentenced to do social work, all because she took yogurt from a supermarket dumpster."

It turns out to be a lucky night for Peter and me, meaning we don't get caught. Even Hardy is astonished when I surprise him with two plastic bags full of food.

The next day, I decide it's time to go to work. I stand in the city's main pedestrian area holding a rather enticing handmade sign: *A butler for a train ticket*. In order to make my offer more attractive, I'm dressed up as an English butler with a bow tie, white shirt with starched collar, button-down vest, black trousers, and white gloves, all of which I had purchased from a second-hand shop (for just 15 Euros!) before leaving Berlin. Who could resist my impeccable butlership?

I expect more of a reaction—any kind of reaction—from the people of Cologne. However, the residents appear to be no longer easily amused, thanks to all the hidden-camera antics and wacky street performers that have begun to take root in the city. After an hour with no success, I decide to take control of the situation and address the passersby directly.

"A train ticket to Belgium in exchange for the best butler in the world!" I confidently exclaim to an old lady who crosses my path, bowing slightly to demonstrate my charm.

"I am in no mood for a circus today!" she retorts, adding a few arm gestures for emphasis.

The embarrassing confrontations continue until I approach one of the more interesting-looking citizens of Cologne, a man I soon learn is named Harold who is 49 years old, but eternally young at heart. Against his suntanned skin he wears a white, open, laced-up vest tucked into tight pants, a look that is finished off neatly with a pair of snakeskin boots. His thinning blond hair is long and partly covered by a headband. He likes my idea, and for the rest of the day, books me as his personal butler.

When we arrive at his place, the first thing I see is a red Ferrari parked in front of his house—or, to put it better, in front of his property. Harold tells me that he bought the car in the 90s for 400,000 Deutschmarks (DM), the old currency of Germany. Now, I am not a car fanatic by any means, but I'm still impressed with an actual *Ferrari*.

Harold quickly thrusts a sponge and cloth into my hand saying, "Now wash the car until it's spic-and-span!" Dutifully, I place the cleaning rag against the rim in order to make it shine, sending Harold into a complete panic.

"Be careful! Ferraris have been damaged from being cleaned in the wrong way! Do it gently! Never, ever on the same spot for too long!" Harold knows exactly what he wants. Hopefully, I won't get sued. A butler's life must be full of incalculable risks.

Two hours later Harold takes me to his garage, which is actually a separate portion of a public parking block. In the garage there are many, many more luxury vehicles: shiny Lamborghinis, gleaming Corvettes, majestic Cadillacs...am I dreaming, or have I, in fact, hooked up with the Russian mafia?

Harold selects a Cadillac convertible from the seventies that must be at least sixteen feet long. I then chauffeur him throughout downtown Cologne, despite the challenge of taking curves with this gigantic car. After successfully parking the Cadillac, we dine at a fancy restaurant...or, to be more accurate, Harold dines while I keep replenishing his wine glass. Again and again during the course of the evening, various women approach our table. Harold seems to attract a certain type of woman; the kind who is even willing to kiss his eccentric boots for a bit of his attention.

They look right through me. I continue pouring wine for Harold.

The remainder of my day as Harold's butler passes quite amusingly. Unfortunately, I never do find out how Harold has made his vast fortune. He tells me that he has no money, but lives only from objects of value. The twenty sports cars he has parked in his garage have already assured me of this. After finishing my duties, Harold invites me to Marbella, Spain, for the coming week, and adds a cryptic tag:

"You could marry well there."

Though I'm curious to know what he means, I know it is time to press on. I politely decline his intriguing invitation and receive 55 Euros for my pay: exactly enough money for a ticket to Antwerp, Belgium. Thankfully, it also means that I will be able to make my free passage to Canada, something that was more difficult to find than I had anticipated.

EU (European Union) law not only discourages, but prohibits anyone's romantic notions of becoming a sailor; luckily, I know a solid man by the name of Peter Doehle whose shipping company rather enterprisingly offers a certain brand of tourist the option of traveling on a container ship. Since he considers my project quite exciting, he is allowing me to travel free of cost.

On the train ride to Belgium, I decide to save my 55 Euros for later and don't buy a ticket. My brilliant plan is to hide in the restroom for the entire trip. I can already visualize myself triumphantly disembarking from the train in Antwerp with 55 Euros still in my pocket, not having spent a single cent. While hidden in the toilet, I smile and congratulate myself on my genius plan until I hear the frantic knocking on the door. Caught by the conductor I not only have to pay the normal fare but also a penalty fee to boot, meaning that I arrive in Brussels with only one Euro left.

Everything up to now has been going so well, but then I tried to be too clever. As a result, I'm now stuck here in Brussels with no idea of how to get to Antwerp. My backpack feels even heavier on my burdened shoulders. I am not sure of what to do, when I suddenly think of one solution: I will board the next train to Antwerp and use the blind-spot trick.

Yes, the blind-spot trick.

I go immediately to the last compartment, which is only about ten by twelve feet, containing only six folding seats. In most of the local trains, the bicycles are usually kept here. I put my backpack in the left corner that faces the other compartments, and stand motionless in the right corner facing the same direction. Normally, the conductors only glance through the window of this compartment's door, and if they don't see anyone, they move on, not thinking to check the blind spots.

(Ladies and gentlemen: the blind-spot trick.)

I spend the rest of the journey tensely pushed up against the right corner of the compartment. Suddenly, the door opens and I have only one thought: *Busted again!* It is not the conductor, or any sort of train official, but a waiter coming through with the coffee cart.

The young man observes me standing there scrunched up in the corner. We both stand there looking at each other for a few seconds without saying a word.

I keep looking at him. He looks right back at me. I think we're saying things with our minds, but I can't be too sure.

I nonchalantly try to act as if I'm just standing there to gaze out of the window, perhaps even propping my chin up on my fist and managing a small smile. The young waiter pushes his coffee cart to the other side of the compartment and proceeds to fix himself some lemonade while keeping his eyes on me—he knows exactly what's going on. I continue staring out the window with an expression of wonder, though I'm not paying a bit of attention to the scenery.

After a few minutes, the waiter pushes the coffee cart back out of the compartment, barely hiding a smile. I arrive in Antwerp both overjoyed by success, and utterly exhausted from holding myself in that position for almost an hour.

My next challenge is to find some food. What if I approach, say, five different shops, and simply explain to them that I am traveling to the end of the world without any money and ask if they would donate some food for my cause? How many of them do will say yes? It's worth a try. So I first approach a nice café run by a young man. He thinks my adventure sounds great, and offers me a coffee and a muffin. The Latin American music playing in the background only increases my anticipation for traveling throughout South America. I then go to a hotel where I manage to refill my two-liter bottle with tap water without any trouble. At my next stop, a fish store, the saleswoman must refuse my request since her boss isn't there to make the decision.

The fourth place I try is a bakery where the employees are very generous: slices of quiche, various buns, some bread, and pastries are packed up and handed to me. The three employees have fun debating which one of them will accompany me on my trip. Finally, a fruit vendor gives me two apples. With four out of five of my requests met with success, I'm left feeling hopeful about the rest of my journey.

2/ All Hands Below Deck
(Antwerp to Montreal)

My new life XXL: Passage to Canada

Antwerp's harbor is about 16 miles long and quite difficult to explore on foot. All around there are trucks driving and numerous cranes incessantly loading and unloading the huge container ships that come from all over the world. Everything must be done quickly, as there's no time to lose. After much searching, I finally find my ship and I'm immediately filled with a sense of adventure.

The *MS Valentina* is 194 yards long and loaded with 1,800 containers. This equals about 22 million gallons; if you think about it in another way, this equals about 86 million liters of beer, or 365 million cups of coffee, or 7.1 billion spoons of sugar. I feel quite humbled in its presence.

Upon entering the ship, I am politely greeted by a Filipino steward: "Hello, Mr. Wigge." He introduces himself as Julius and brings me to my cabin. To my astonishment, he insists on carrying my backpack although it's quite heavy and almost as big as he is. I'll be spending the next twelve days in a comfortable sleeping cabin that includes a small private lounge with a stereo system, a satellite television with over 900 channels, and a minibar. Julius tells me that I can always reach him on the ship's phone system—"Extension 148!"—then politely takes his leave. I sit on my bed feeling unbelievably happy, for I had never expected to find such luxury on a container ship.

I meet Julius again while I'm having a look around the ship, and he tells me that meals are at eight o'clock in the morning, noon, and five in the evening, but that it's not a problem if I'm a little late. Near the dining hall is a fitness area, and beyond that is the ship's cinema, stocked with plenty of DVDs. Julius proudly goes over everything, explaining, "Our passengers should be happy!" I realize that they must have booked me as a tourist and not as a helper, as was discussed on the phone, but I certainly am not going to be the one to complain. Thus, my journey across the Atlantic will be made in unexpected comfort.

There is plenty to eat. I listen to the news on the BBC, Russia Today, France 24, Deutsche Welle, and Al Jazeera, comparing the different views of each one. I enthusiastically begin selecting DVDs to watch over the next twelve days: *Casino* to prepare myself for Las Vegas, *Back to the Future* to relive memories of my childhood, all three parts of *The Lord of the Rings* so that I wouldn't be the only one to have not seen this trilogy, and classics featuring Joe Pesci and Al Pacino. Just as I'm reaching out to grab the Steve Buscemi film *The Interview*, the German captain, Mr. Kamrad, approaches me.

"Mr. Wigge, I've just heard that we have an extra helper on board!" His smile is massive. It is not unlike having a bucket of ice-cold water dumped over me in order to wake me from my dream. I keep my cool and simply ask him how I may help.

For the rest of the journey, I become a proper sailor. Every morning I get up at six, put on my work gear, and sorrowfully glance back at the stack of 35 DVDs, waiting to be watched in my cabin. My work schedule unfolds as such: on Monday I paint the railings of the ship with a fellow named Ramir, while waves 15 to 20 feet high rise up all around us. On Tuesday I help do inventory of all of the food and supplies. On Wednesday I accompany a man named Victor to check the cooling systems, requiring us to go 70 feet above deck and look down into the never-ending chasms of the 1,800 containers, all stacked on top of the other at least five or seven times. On Thursday I am on the bridge with the captain. On Friday I'm with the chief engineer in the engine room where the main engine has a power of 23000 HP (note: that would be approximately 50 of Harold's Ferraris) and needs about 425 gallons of oil.

For me, a successful oil change on my car brings me vast amounts of pleasure, so I can already imagine how much I'm going to enjoy an oil change on *MS Valentina*. Even though I'm only allowed to change the oil of an auxiliary engine, the procedure is much the same: I unscrew the caps, lid, filters and filter safeguards; I lay them out in the order I remove them so that I know in which sequence they are replaced; I pay attention to how the heat regulates itself so that there are no burns; I unclear any and all clumps from the 20-series Allen key; I take out the oil filter with a myriad of devices; I let the old oil drain out before putting in new oil; and finally, I reassemble everything. The satisfaction this brings me is immense.

During those twelve days aboard the ship, it occurs to me that the entire 20-member crew—the captain, the officers, the engineers, the cook, the helpers, and even the steward—all have a strictly regulated routine. Everyone knows exactly what he has to do, and everything operates without anyone having to say anything. What's more, the people are very polite to one another, there is never any tension or bickering, and after completing the day's work, everyone retreats to his cabin.

This is, quite frankly, nothing like how I imagined seafaring people to be. I had romantically envisioned gruff, six-and-a-half-feet tall, tattooed Russian sailors living in dark, dingy cabins below the deck, playing vicious games of cards every night while pounding back endless quantities of vodka. In fact, when I had arranged the trip with the shipping company, I had even mentioned that I would like to sleep with the sailors below the deck. (The stoic Mr. Doehle must have thought that journalists have a tendency to exaggerate, and didn't say anything further about my offer.) Before my departure, I had asked myself how the sailors would react when they came to offer me vodka, only to find out that I don't drink, but I now see, much to my shock, that no one drinks alcohol here at all. Well, maybe with one exception, on one night…

On Saturday evening, the ship's cook, Capriano, organizes a grill party where steaks, chicken drumsticks, and spareribs are laid out on the table of the dining hall. I sit with the captain and the officers and we talk about the ship hijackings off the coast of Somalia. I, of course, waste no time and begin spouting off all of my expertise, points of view, and opinions as a journalist while they listen indulgently.

All of a sudden, the stereo system behind me starts playing *"Lambang Layassayh, Lamam Hanang."* I turn around to see my fellow sailor, Ramir, vociferously singing karaoke to a Filipino love song. Accompanying him is a video clip of bikini-clad babes (judging by their hair, from the mid-80s) running along the beaches of Malibu. The captain grins and says that 11 of the 20 sailors are from the Philippines, and so they have a great fondness for love songs from their country. Ramir appears to be feeling little to no pain, and is completely immersed in his rather admirable rendition of the tune.

Images of Ramir from the last few days spring to my mind. Every day he calmly paints the handrails of the ship for ten hours a day, while 20-foot waves occasionally rise up over the deck. I know that he is away from his family during the six to eight months of his contract, working six-and-a-half days every week, getting only half of his Sundays free. The only entertainment is karaoke on Saturdays and, on rare occasions, a brief shore leave.

Viktor, a Ukrainian who works in the engine room, has revealed to me that the best part of his job is that it feels like he's on vacation for six to eight months. Since he's away for such long periods, he's able to enjoy his time at home more with his wife and family without the usual stress. It's the first time I've been acquainted with this type of lifestyle, and so I'm lost in my thoughts, until

"The Time of my Life" from *Dirty Dancing* starts playing on the karaoke machine and I'm swiftly brought back to reality. I quickly jump up and grab the microphone.

3/ True North, Land of the Free (Montreal to Niagara)

Walking on sunshine: Olympic Stadium, Montreal

After 12 days at sea, we arrive in Montreal's harbor, and I once again, mercifully, have solid ground underneath my feet. I am officially in Canada.

Some citizens of the neighboring United States enviously look to the rights that all Canadians have, and even sometimes refer to it as the "land of the free", a rather ironic nickname as it is taken from their very own American national anthem. A public healthcare system, legal same-sex marriage, abortion rights, low poverty and crime rates, and an abolished death penalty are achievements that the Canadian people can be proud of.

Through www.couchsurfing.com I meet Raphaelle and Jessie, with whom I will stay for the coming days. For those unacquainted with the service, Couchsurfing.com is a global social networking community where people offer backpackers their couch for a free night's stay. The basic premise is that you create a profile with a description of your personality, and then you can either search for, or post a place, one that is rated by other travelers who have stayed there.

In the past, I have let couch surfers stay in my apartment who came from all over the world and who all turned out to be very interesting and kind: guitar hippies from Sweden, a couple from California who were on a world tour, and, most recently, an intern from Senegal named Ken who was excited to stay with me because he had seen me on television. (My report series, *The Truth about Germany*, is aired on Deutsche Welle TV, which broadcasts in 160 countries. Ken claims that his German has improved by watching my series, and actually knew 50 of the 65 episodes by heart.)

I also occasionally take advantage of this network and stay overnight with some couch surfer hosts, mostly when I am traveling for Deutsche Welle.

When traveling, I always bring my small netbook so that I'm easily able to contact my respective hosts. Despite the extra weight, when I'm already weighed down with my backpack and video equipment, its hardware allows me to surf the net for free wherever there is free Wi-Fi. Since cyber-cafés cost money and I don't have any, I'm more than thankful for all of the free networks available in North America. The website www.wififreespot.com even seems to think that the number of free networks here is inexhaustible.

...but back to Raphaelle and Jessie, the two girls I will be staying with: they live in a two-bedroom apartment in the eastern part of Montreal, both 29 years old and very attractive. A lot of couch surfers have already passed through their bright, friendly apartment, which is kept minimally furnished but still quite stylish. Since neither of them travels much, they are very happy to have guests and get to know people from other countries.

My first evening at their place, we all sit around their kitchen table exchanging stories. Raphaelle, a fashion designer who loves colorful stripes in her designs, is enthusiastic about my travel attempt. Jessie, who works as a kindergarten teacher, is curious to know all about my trip up to this point. As I begin to elaborate, my stomach once again interrupts with a growling noise, but Raphaelle and Jessie are far too excited and engrossed in my storytelling to hear it.

Instead of being impolite and asking for something to eat, I would rather wait until they offer me something. Unfortunately, I wait in vain, as the girls are much too fascinated by my travel stories to realize that I may be hungry (and without money). Finally it gets to the point where Jessie can no longer ignore the growling of my stomach, so she places a bowl of cookies on the table and offers them to me. The cookies are large and round and sugary-looking, resembling those of the sandwich-chain Subway: in other words, just the right thing to satisfy my hunger.

Greedily, I grab the cookies and quickly shove three of them, one by one, in my mouth. Delicious. Raphaelle and Jessie both look at me wide-eyed. What is it? Am I being impolite? No, that isn't it. Jessie calmly offers me by way of explanation: "These are *space cookies,* so you really shouldn't eat too many."

"Space cookies"? Space...is she talking about *hash* cookies? Alarmed, I put the fourth one down just as I'm about to put it into my mouth. For this trip I had given up smoking and wouldn't be drinking any alcohol, so this is the last thing I need. Gradually, a warm, fuzzy feeling slowly works over me, and I begin to wonder if I can manage a free visit to the Betty Ford clinic during my trip.

At this moment, the doorbell rings and Felix, a good acquaintance of the girls, comes in. It turns out that Felix is much like a best friend and stylist to the girls. He cuts their hair and advises them how to dress when they go out in the evening. Today, Jessie ignores his suggestion of the white summer dress with black polka dots and, instead, wears something a bit more subtle. Felix doesn't mind, as it just means that he can wear the dress instead.

A little later Felix is standing in front of the mirror wearing the dress and proceeds to stick out his butt proudly. I don't know whether it's the space cookies working their magic or just that the situation is so funny, but I suddenly can't stop laughing. Felix is six foot two, broad and lean. I wonder, if I squeezed into a schoolgirl's outfit, whether I could pull it off as well as Felix.

A while later (five minutes? Five hours?) we are in Raphaelle's car and I am sitting in the backseat beside Felix, who is still wearing the dress. He only gives me a grin but it's enough to make me start laughing again. Apparently the space cookies must still be working since Jessie, Raphaelle and Felix can't understand what is so funny. We drive up the 765-foot-high hill called Mont Royal, from which the city gets its name. The view from there is breathtaking. The skyline is brightly lit under the night sky and one can see both the skyscrapers downtown, as well as the old city with its alleys and houses reminiscent of Paris.

Raphaelle and Jessie tell me that Montreal is, linguistically, a divided city. Raphaelle points out the area just to the left of the old city where French is mainly spoken, and the area to its right where only English is spoken. This divide dates back to when the French immigrants founded the city in the 17th century. However, in the struggle for supremacy in North America, the British were victorious, and all of Canada came under British rule in 1763 despite this province being inhabited only by French settlers.

From 1844 to 1849, Montreal was the capital city of the British colony, bringing a whole new wave of English immigrants which led to the division of the city between French and English. The official language of Quebec is French: shops are obliged to tag their goods in French; all signage is written in the mother tongue of Céline Dion; and there is even an alarmingly-named *language police* who monitor the compliance with these regulations.

Raphaelle, in her strongly French-accented English, tells me that the citizens of Quebec are increasingly demanding complete freedom from Canada because they feel discriminated against by the Canadian government. Jessie, on the other hand, comes from Ontario and considers the demand for independence quite unnecessary and arrogant. While discussing this social issue, it becomes clear how very different the two girls' viewpoints are, and how quickly the tension builds when discussing this topic. Despite all this, they make a good example of city's English-French integration and how harmonious relations are, in fact, possible.

I slowly begin to notice that the others are equally as stoned as I am, because the topic abruptly changes and we begin laughing over everything—even at Quebec's perpetual drive for independence. We speak by mingling our French, English and German, and all magically understand each other. Luckily, the language police are not on patrol this night.

In order to avoid eating more space cookies in the days to come, I head off the next morning to get some food for myself. After my positive experience with dumpster diving in Cologne, I decide to give it a try here in Montreal. However, the aroma coming from the bakeries and the tempting food on display in their windows spoils my motivation. Instead, I again decide to ask the shops for free food. To my great relief, I have surprisingly good results and my food supply for the next few days is quickly secured.

Now I must face my next problem: how am I supposed to continue my journey from Montreal without a single penny in my pocket? The only possibility is the long-distance bus, but it costs money that I don't have. Early the next morning, I go to the bus station filled with a sense of anxiety and concern that, if I don't succeed, I'll have to sheepishly go back to Raphaelle and Jessie's place.

At the bus terminal I talk to the manager of Coach Canada. She finds my stories bewildering, but amusing as well. I talk, she laughs, and I turn up the charm.

Then, abruptly, she says, "What do you really want from me?"

So I tell her: a free ticket to Niagara Falls. She is astonished at my honesty but not at all annoyed. "In my eleven years as manager for Coach Canada," she says, "no one has ever asked me for a free trip. I'll see what I can do." She takes me to her colleague Bill, who promptly issues me a free ticket for the nine-hour trip. Bill then shakes my hand and wishes me all the best for my journey.

I feel extremely happy and lucky when I arrive later that evening in the town of St. Catharines (where Niagara Falls is located). It's there that I continue my couch surfing by spending two nights with Nicole, a teacher in her early 30s who lives in a house with her two cats. Apart from her book club, she appears to hardly have any contact with other people, so couch surfers are a welcome opportunity for her to get to know other people and socialize, which makes perfect sense to me.

However, we do not seem to share any common interests and I can't help but feel that the atmosphere is somehow too formal. On my first evening at her house, we sit more or less quietly in her kitchen, and then Nicole offers to prepare some food for us. When I first offer to help she declines, but she finally gives in when I refuse to be dissuaded. It doesn't take long, though, before she is raising her eyebrows; apparently, I am not cutting the vegetables properly. I even begin to doubt myself and, accidentally, drop a carrot on the floor. That's more than enough to make Nicole request in a friendly but firm manner that I wait in the living room. I offer to at least set the table, but seeing her appalled look I instead go sit in the living room and play with the two cats.

Breakfast the next morning is also quiet. Nicole suddenly breaks the silence by mentioning the English comedian Sacha Baron Cohen, who is famous for his roles as Ali G, Borat and Brüno. I'm relieved to finally find something in common we can talk about, and begin repeating lines from his films and telling her how awesome and funny I think he is. Sacha Baron Cohen! A comedic genius!

"I find him flippant," says Nicole abruptly.

"I don't like him either," I meekly respond.

In the evening I come back from wandering around town and proudly show her the apples, bananas and sandwiches that various shops gave me for free. Nicole just gives me a skeptical look which clearly tells me that this isn't a way she would ever go about getting food.

Putting our differences aside, the next day Nicole invites me to go with her to see Niagara Falls. Comprised of two waterfalls approximately 3,937 feet wide, about two-thirds of which lie in Canada and one-third in the U.S., seeing them in person is overwhelming (and, thankfully, free). We manage to get unbelievably close, close enough to take good photos.

Nicole and decide to ride the boat that goes directly beneath the falls. When we get to the ticket booth, I see that two tickets cost 29 dollars. I present my usual spiel to the ticket saleswoman about being a reporter who is traveling to the end of the world without money, and then brazenly ask her if I can take the boat ride for free. The woman briefly looks over the papers I hand her that confirm my itinerary, waves Nicole and me through, and wishes both *my assistant* and I a nice boat ride. Nicole tensely watches me the entire time I'm talking and clearly doesn't approve of this approach, but she's also equally impressed that we get to ride the boat for free.

The boat ride soon changes the mood. Before us, water pours from 165 feet above and makes the tourists slide all around, screaming with either delight or terror. Directly in front of the falls we can only see a solid white wall and hear the hellish, deafening roar of the water. Both Nicole and I are completely enthralled. That evening, perhaps elevated by the excitement of the day's adventure, she offers to drive me the next day across the American border to Cleveland, which is about 220 miles away. Lost for words, I offer her a hug of gratitude and, for the first time, see the beginnings of a smile on her face.

At the U.S. border, we are successfully directed out of Canada. I have to explain to the immigration office why I am entering the United States without any type of return ticket, already quite aware from past experience that entering the U.S. would not be a walk in the park.

Back in 1997, I had an encounter with customs when I was living in California for a year. For spring break, my friends and I decided to go to Mexico. On our return I had difficulty re-entering as I had only brought my American driver's license, but the border officer wanted to see my passport, which my friends were supposed to have faxed overnight to the immigration office. After waiting for hours, all of us had to pay a fine of 100 dollars before we were allowed to continue with our journey.

This time, the female officer looks over the official details of my end-of-the-world-without-money concept, makes further inquiries, and then decides to let me enter the country without a return ticket for a fine of only six dollars. Nicole, who is breathing tensely beside me, is probably already having second thoughts about taking me with her, and signals me to quickly pay the fine. However, as I do not have a single cent, the officer only gives me an irritated look and goes to get her boss.

He reads through my concept, looks directly at me, and says in a strict tone, "Sir, you *will not* enter the United States of America!" Stunned, devastated and shocked, I try to think of what I'm going to do now. But within seconds—though seeming much longer to me—the supervisor laughs and tells me that I can enter and that it sounds like a cool project. This is what I can only surmise as being "border humor". Nicole and I are both ecstatic, and I can tell that the anarchic nature of our success makes her happy.

Once we get to Cleveland, we make a visit to the art museum, as it has free entry. We then bid each other farewell, and I can't thank her enough for her hospitality.

4/ Go West, Young Man
(Cleveland to New Mexico)

No bed in the cornfield: on the way in Ohio

I am standing near an on-ramp at the edge of Cleveland holding a large cardboard sign that reads, quite simply, *SOUTH*. Luckily, I still have no idea what is in store for me in the coming weeks.

Hitchhiking here appears to be more difficult than in Germany. Although not prohibited officially, it is no longer in fashion. Gone are the times when one could experience adventures like those of Jack Kerouac. Today, a man standing with an outstretched thumb on the road is only looked at with suspicion. Nevertheless, except on freeways, it is still technically legal.

On average about eleven cars go past me every minute, but not one of them stops. I spend a good eight hours in the same spot until an old couple traveling to the Hamburger Festival in Akron finally picks me up. But Akron isn't that far, and after a short while I'm stranded at the Hamburger Festival where, unbelievably, no one is willing to even donate a solitary hamburger to my cause. So, using the few dollars that I received as a gift from Nicole, I take the bus to the neighboring city of Canton.

On the bus I soon get into a conversation with Harold, an African-American man around my age. He is excited about my journey and keeps crying out, "It's so amazing, man. You're so cool. I can't believe that I've met you!" He tells me that he has two kids in Miami from his first wife and two kids from his second wife, who lives in a trailer park just outside of Canton. Suddenly Harold invites me to spend the night with him and his girlfriend. Everything happens quite quickly and, spontaneously, I agree and get off at the next stop with him.

As we make our way to the trailer park, Harold calls his girlfriend to excitedly announce my arrival. But he then becomes quiet and I can tell that her reply doesn't make him happy. He finally interrupts her and furiously yells into the phone: "Hold on, relax, pull back!" But not letting him speak, he suddenly begins shouting at her into the receiver: "Shut up, you fucking bitch! Shut finally the fuck UP!"

It is then that I realize I won't be staying at their place for the night, and try to make Harold aware of this by hand gesturing. He moves the phone away from his ear and gives me a huge smile. "She's only a little drunk…it will all work out." He then goes back to swearing and hurling abuse at her, using English slang that I have never, ever heard before. I turn around and wave once again to let him know that I'm leaving. How could I be so careless? I suppose the whole thing could have ended much worse.

I wander on a country road, somewhere in Ohio, facing the evening sun. I decide to keep going for a while until something happens. But the only thing that happens is that it becomes very dark, so I set up my tent behind a McDonald's and sleep under the star-filled sky of Ohio.

The next day I keep moving along the road, my backpack weighing nearly 88 pounds. I start to walk more and more slowly, and it begins to feel as if I'm pulling against a huge rubber band that is tied to my backpack. I wander through a beautiful stretch countryside full of small hills, alleys and farms until later that afternoon when Mickey, a rocker girl around 40 years old with a cigarette stub balanced in her mouth and a leather jacket on her shoulders, takes me along for a few miles in an old van. She talks very patriotically about her part of the country and comes quickly to the point: "It's a nice area because there are no black people living here."

"What is the problem with black people?" I ask tentatively.

"No worries, I do like them, as long as they don't live in my area."

I have arrived in the legendary Midwest of the USA, the part of the country where every foreigner is first under suspicion. The locals apparently leave liberal thinking and open-mindedness to those *maniacs* on the West Coast; here, they prefer to stay conservative. I grow rather uneasy and I'm immediately reminded of a report project my buddy and I wanted to do during our film school days in London, where the basic idea was that I act as a reporter and ask people on the street for various favors. The next day, I would do the exact same thing, only as a person of African descent, and we would then compare the results. To change the color of my face and skin, we thought of applying shoe polish or chocolate cream—an experiment in blackface that is embarrassingly naïve in retrospect. The project, unsurprisingly, was shelved, as our film professor found it to be beyond politically incorrect.

A few hours later, after being dropped off by Mickey, the number of cars passing me become fewer as the traffic of black horse-drawn carriages increases—carriages carrying members of the Amish community.

The Amish are not allowed to use cars, and live almost as if they were in the 18th century. Men wear straw hats, full beards, and suspenders on their pants; women wear white bonnets, plain or conservative clothing, and no make-up. They place emphasis on family, community, and seclusion from the outside world. Today, they live in 1,200 colonies in 26 American states. They lead their lives in the countryside, are known for rejecting modern technology, and only accept some innovations after careful thought.

I try to stop a carriage with my thumb, but the members of the Amish community react as indifferently as the 5,000 car drivers did in Cleveland yesterday. I become even more exhausted and ask myself where this trip is actually taking me. I will certainly never be able to reach Antarctica this way. The first doubts begin to creep into my mind about actually being able to accomplish this project.

At around two in the afternoon, I finish the last of my water and continue to be ignored by the carriages—even my efforts at waving, hopping, laughing out loud, and making funny grimaces don't stop them. After walking for about six miles with my unrelenting backpack, I finally start to physically break down. The afternoon sun is shining down on me and I'm dehydrated. I have to stop every 500 yards and take off backpack to rest.

In an earnest effort to pump myself up, I turn on my MP3 player and listen to "The Greatest Party in History" by Kante, vaguely aware that there probably is no place where *the greatest party* could be further from than Amish county in Ohio. (I later read that no alcohol can be served in the entire county and that the Amish refrain from modern forms of entertainment like music, television, and the internet.) A short while later, the German singer Peter Fox is roaring in my ear with strong bass tones, singing mightily about cocaine, needles, how Tarek wants to punch Sam, and about how "blood splashes". While I'm listening to this, I see Amish kids by the roadside and adults and families on their way to the church. Along with my extreme fatigue, this audio-visual mix creates a very surreal music video.

At this point, I can probably manage only one more mile before I fall down by the side of the road in a state of complete exhaustion. My head is spinning, I'm overheated, and I need water badly. Although I have given up hope by now, I still squat on the roadside and hold my thumb out to the carriages passing by. Astonishingly, an Amish man stops his carriage and offers to take me to his farm.

"Thank you," I somehow manage to croak. He smiles back at me in reply.

As we drive, we approach a town sign that says *Berlin*, and I literally rub my eyes to make sure I have read this correctly. Am I hallucinating? Did I lose consciousness and get sent back to Germany? It would, somehow, be amusing if I really did get driven back to Berlin in a horse-drawn carriage. Mark, the driver, seems to have read my thoughts and begins explaining that the Amish are Christians who get baptized between the ages of 16 and 20 years old, and then proceeds to give me a short history lesson detailing his heritage.

When the Christian reform movement arose in the 17th century, they were put at a disadvantage in many parts of Europe where the rules did not accept the Amish refusal to do military service and swear an oath. They were persecuted by authorities and finally forced to migrate to the new world. Since the Amish originally came from the region of Europe where German is spoken, they gave names like Berlin and Hamburg to their new colonies in America, something that I find genuinely fascinating.

Changing the subject, Mark cheerfully asks me what I'm doing here. "Why aren't you cultivating your land at home?"

"It didn't go so well with the land," I reply.

"Now I understand why you don't have any money." Then he offers me his barn to stay in for the night, an offer I gratefully accept.

Over the next few days, his wife Elizabeth and his brother Ernie make sure that I am properly fed and rested; it actually takes me three full days to fully recover from my exhaustion and near-dehydration. Once I am restored to health, I offer to help with the field work in order to thank them for their kindness and hospitality. Perhaps this isn't enough, since Mark instead suggests that I sweep the stalls. It's a job that is usually done by the women in the village, but I am happy to do anything to show my appreciation and gratitude for their astounding generosity.

Ernie has seven kids with his wife, which is about average here. During mealtimes, all of the kids—who range in age from three to fourteen years old—sit well-mannered at the table. There is no jumping, screaming, complaining or talking. It's a disciplined atmosphere, but also relaxed with the father and the mother talking. Before our first meal together begins, Ernie reads aloud a benediction from the Bible in German. I'm flabbergasted. Although their language is an old German dialect, which I understand only partly, the prayers themselves are said in standard German.

Mark and his wife, Elizabeth, live in a nearby house. When I first see Elizabeth, I have to wonder if I have landed on a Hollywood set and, like Harrison Ford, am actually searching for the *witness*. Basically, Elisabeth looks a lot like Angelina Jolie, and I have to ask myself why such an attractive, eloquent young woman is leading this rustic kind of life.

Elisabeth married Mark when she was 19 years old and she does everything in the household, raises the kids, and has never traveled more than six miles with her carriage. When we are lighting the gas lanterns one evening, Elizabeth tells me that she is happy and has never thought about another kind of life.

This makes me remember a conversation I had had with Karthik, an Indian physicist who took in both Nicole and me as couch surfers for one night in Cleveland. The main discussion that evening had been how we in western society have so many choices, that it in return makes us unhappy. He put forward the argument that arranged marriages have the advantage of not giving people very high expectations. Naturally, I had disagreed with this. However, while I am wandering through Ohio this one evening, I begin to think about my own life as a bachelor: the party acquaintances, the women I know through work or through my group of friends, plus the new contacts I make through online dating. Within one month I could get to know about twenty women, yet I had never fallen in love with any of them.

So who's happier? I think.

After my few days of recuperating in this Amish paradise, Mark gives me his bicycle for my journey. At first I don't want to accept it, but Mark insists that it's my salary for my work, and also shows me in which direction to head if I want to go west. I'm happy and excited about my impending bike trip through the idyllic landscape of Ohio. Upon saying goodbye to Ernie, he gives me a Bible, enough food for the next few days, and, unbelievably, a 100-dollar bill. I'm totally speechless. Mark urges me to take the money: "You have worked for it. Take it for a bus ticket. Or do you want to travel to Antarctica with the bicycle?" I laugh and recall my very first impression of the Amish as being unfamiliar with the outside world.

Cycling with 88 pounds on my back is—how do I describe it?—not fun. After an hour, the gearshift on my bike breaks so that I can only cycle in sixth gear. The region is very uneven and the entire day consists of me riding uphill and downhill, so my progress is very slow. My water disappears by the early afternoon. I ask an old lady standing in front of her house whether I can get some tap water from somewhere. Wordlessly, she points in the direction of Danville, which is three miles away, and turns back to her house.

These three miles are, again, uphill, so I really must push, but I'd much rather just pedal. I just want to get to the end of it. I feel like I'm getting into an anaerobic situation; my body consumes more oxygen than it is getting. I know this feeling quite well from the thousand-meter races that I participated in when I was younger. My body is aching and my oxygen is low, but I must persevere until my body pumps out so much adrenaline that I no longer feel any pain…and so, while climbing up towards Danville, I find myself in this state for the first time in 15 years.

After about two more miles I no longer feel any pain and I start pedaling with full force. Sweat is pouring from my whole body, but I keep going. I travel almost 56 miles this day. Sometime later I come to an area with farmhouses close to the road. I stop and talk to a calm, white-haired man in jeans who is repairing old cars in his garage. He listens to my story with interest, but hesitates when I ask him if I could spend the night camping on his land. For that he must first speak to his wife.

Even without hearing what he and his wife say, it's obvious that this question allows for a lengthy discussion between the two. Matthew and Deborah first offer me water and, after eyeing me suspiciously for a while, finally decide to let me set up my tent behind their house for the night. I immediately conclude that the retired couple leads a very secluded life in their small white house: while Matthew works a lot on his cars, Deborah is completely absorbed in the maintenance of her garden and reads the Bible a lot.

That evening I sit with Matthew on his terrace and we exchange travel stories. He tells me of his experiences of traveling through the U.S. in the sixties and sleeping in the back of his Chevy box van in the parking lots of supermarkets, and I can't help but notice how my presence seems to re-energize him. Eventually he even takes out his guitar and plays old Johnny Cash songs.

The next morning I wake up in my tent but can hardly move: the muscles in my upper and lower legs, back, chest and shoulders are completely stiff. Today, I need to cover the same distance once again in order to make it to the next major city. However, it will be impossible like this. I move and cycle at a snail's pace throughout the day, occasionally cursing the entire trip. I never imagined that my adventure would be like this.

By evening I at last reach the major city of Columbus, population 700,000. I enter the city and find myself in the middle of what appears to be a ghetto. Entire streets of houses are boarded up with plywood, deserted and abandoned, while some buildings are gutted. Along the roadside young Latino and African-American men are casually hanging around. From the land of the Amish straight into a gangster's paradise! They wear undershirts, baggy pants, gold chains and do-rags. Many of them are smoking small pipes; I am fairly sure that it must be crack, though I don't want to jump to conclusions based on what various Hollywood films have portrayed.

At a red traffic light, one of the youths makes a gesture to me which can only interpreted as a hearty *fuck you*. I decide to go through the red light; after all, I seem to be the only white person and only cyclist in the area. Slowly, I feel like I am becoming something of a professional cyclist.

At the Greyhound bus terminal I try to exchange my bicycle for a bus ticket so that I can travel faster and cover more distance to the west. The 100 dollars that Ernie gave me is still not sufficient for a ticket to New Mexico. The assistant, supervisor, and manager do not show any interest in my traveling-without-money tales. They don't even care enough to want to hear about the concept. What's going on here? Everywhere else people have been very enthusiastic about my story.

In the waiting area of the terminal, the atmosphere is anything but comforting. A woman is screaming at the ticket seller. A man curses at the screaming woman. A strung-out Mexican guy runs completely mad through the terminal while provoking other travelers. Finally, an employee advises me to go to the organization called First Link. Apparently, at First Link they help pay for the tickets of needy travelers.

When I get there, a lady who seems to love meeting new people greets me. She talks and talks and does not let me utter a word. She talks about First Link, her role there, surely exaggerating how many people have gotten help in Columbus, and so on, without ever coming to the point of why I'm there. Eventually she thrusts something resembling a phone directory in my hand, which contains the numbers of the organizations I am supposed to call. I try to explain to her again that without money I cannot make any of these phone calls. She still doesn't seem to understand or care, so I go back to the terminal and try again to talk to the manager, Mike. I call him *Little Mike,* like I hear his colleagues doing, because he is only five feet tall. I try to convince him to take the money I have and the bicycle in return for a ticket to the West Coast.

Little Mike merely has me thrown out of his office.

I finally manage to sell the mountain bike for 40 dollars at a second-hand bike shop. The money I now have suffices to buy a bus ticket to Albuquerque, New Mexico—a distance of about 1,500 miles, but I will now be able cover it all in just mere hours. Finally I am making some headway!

I quickly run through the shops downtown and ask for food. The success rate is surprisingly high: 80 percent, just like in Antwerp and Montreal, something I didn't expect in this city after my recent experiences. Of the 20 shops I visit, 16 give me food. The McDonald's on High Street is totally staffed by students of Ohio State University who go completely nuts when I tell them about my trip; they give me a few free burgers and talk about calling the local television station to have me interviewed. However, my bus is waiting at the station, and so I have to walk away from all the fun. I board the Greyhound coach with my trash bag full of food and relax for the next 35 hours. After all of the cycling and the trekking, any other means of transportation is more than highly-welcomed.

Sitting on the bus doesn't make my body ache or sweat or get sunburned; I am, as they say, a happy camper. The bus takes me through several states and time zones. I see the Gateway Arch in St. Louis, travel through Oklahoma City, and continue to follow the green landscape as it turns into the desert.

5/ All-American Gigolo (Albuquerque)

We arrive in Albuquerque, New Mexico, early Sunday morning. I step off the bus and feel pretty good, given that I have just slept for two hours in some previously-untried acrobatic position. Now it's time to find some food, so I head to the nearest McDonald's. The successful experience I had just two days ago makes it seem promising and fills me with confidence; I instead only get thrown out.

A man standing outside of the door starts to preach about how everyone is accepted in the local Baptist church. I am in no mood to attend a church service; I am hungry, plain and simple. However, he won't let me get rid of him and insists that I meet him at the Noonday Church at, appropriately, noon. Since I haven't much planned for this first day in Albuquerque, and it's slightly less than 95 degrees Fahrenheit in the shade, I reach the church at noon sharp.

There is a line of at least 300 people in front of the church, all filing into the house of the Lord. I can see that the majority of them are homeless. A generous meal of beans and steak is waiting for everyone inside. After a sermon by the priest and a few songs, I devour my lunch within minutes. With a satisfied stomach, I begin to take notice of the characters and scenarios around me.

A wearied woman who looks like she is in her fifties, but whom I learn is, in fact, only in her thirties, has a rubber strip tied around her arm and visible track marks. Behind her is a policeman with a pistol ready in case any violence breaks out. In front of me are two guys who strategically hold newspapers in front of their faces while I am filming with my video camera. The man sitting next to me advises me to pack away my camera immediately, because he suspects that the gentlemen across from us may be wanted criminals.

On the far left side of the main room I also notice some hairdresser's chairs—the very type you'd find in a salon. Apparently, after eating, everyone is entitled to a free haircut. Meanwhile, there's a lottery draw taking place and the names of the winners are announced over the microphone. The prizes are donations by the local shops so they are generally different every day. This is all very new to me, and quite fascinating.

While hanging around in the church, surveying my surroundings, I start up a conversation with 57-year-old Joseph. He has been homeless for almost two years but looks surprisingly well groomed: tennis socks, sports shoes, a clean T-shirt, and a new baseball cap. *How can this person be homeless?* I wonder, as he doesn't fit my mind's stereotype. He invites me to spend the day with him, and I waste no time in accepting his invitation.

While we explore Albuquerque, he shows me the contents in his sports bag: a razor, shaving cream, shampoo, a toothbrush, and other toiletries—all packed in an orderly fashion—along with extra T-shirts and trousers. He also smells considerably more pleasant than the others.

Joseph tells me his life story, about all the events that led him to his current situation, and I listen attentively. I learn that he joined the military when he was 16 years old. Just when he was supposed to be sent to Vietnam, he refused and was sacked. He then got a job as a truck driver and supported his wife and his two kids for 30 years. Eventually his wife could no longer put up with his drinking habit and they divorced. Shortly thereafter, Joseph was let go from his company, and he then became a full-blown alcoholic. His cousin took him in for two years as a sort of babysitter until his cousin's wife kicked him out. Since then he has been sleeping in homeless shelters or on park benches. "The churches in the U.S.," he adds, "take over the responsibility for the poor, whereas in Europe it's taken over by the government."

In the afternoon he shows me his free voicemail box where people can leave messages for him. He also introduces me to the clerics who provide the homeless with opportunities to shower. Finally, a shower. It is very, very much needed after my long bus trip, to say the least. We continue further to the Good Shepherd Mission, where

I can see that a free dinner is offered here in which at least 300 people are trying to get in. However, the seats are limited and the mood feels aggressive. Joseph tells me that many of the needy here have done time in prison.

For the night he offers me three possibilities: first, under the bridge of the city freeway, but I run the risk of being robbed there. Second, I can take a bed in the Good Shepherd Mission. He explains that I have the best chance there because seven nights are allotted to each new visitor. Finally, I can sleep in the park between the military hospital and the military base. The choice is obvious to me since I don't want to get robbed, nor do I want to take a bed away from someone who actually needs it when I'm merely conducting a no-money experiment. "Take me to the park by the hospital," I say.

The hospital is on the outskirts of the city; there are hardly any people in the park at night. Every once in a while we see a couple making out at the nearby parking area, or a truck secretly dumping garbage into the hospital container. I want to set up my tent, but Joseph stops me by waving his hand. He says it is too risky because the police can spot us. I agree and look forward to a warm, open-air night admiring the starry sky.

This optimistic thinking is short-lived; at midnight it starts to rain. There is no chance of staying dry, even after we pull our sleeping bags under the trees. The dampness, the constant fear of getting robbed, and the risk of getting caught by the police all leave my mind exhausted. At one point the thought of taking a bed at the shelter doesn't even feel so bad anymore—at least then we would be dry and with a roof over our heads. Totally drenched, I try to sleep but only manage a mere few hours, and wake up at three in the morning feeling miserable. *How must Joseph feel? Joseph, who has been doing this day in and day out for two years?*

The next morning he tells me that he has hopes to fit back into society because the military will soon be paying out his pension. I want more details, as I get the impression that he has been waiting for this for a very long time. I then have to leave Joseph, and promise to leave a message for him in his voicemail box at the mission, and during our farewell we both have tears in our eyes. It has probably been a while since Joseph has had someone keep him company; I am sad to leave him behind.

At this point in time, I have no idea that I will receive a call from him months later, long after I am back in Berlin, with the great news that he has an apartment and is working again.

Soon, I am heading west towards Las Vegas with Dan in his 1965 Mustang Fastback. The perfect car for a road trip: not only is it easy on the eyes, but it is quiet and purrs like a cat. Women can't help but stare, and men come up to talk to us at gas stations. I found Dan through an advertisement on www.couchsurfing.com. His life is anything but boring: he is 35 years old and, up until three years ago, he served as a pilot for spies in the military. He says that the only way he survived those 18-hour shifts was with caffeine and alcohol. After two years he was so burned out that he decided to leave the service, and so armed with a proper compensation, he then started his career as a day trader. He tells me how he was able to double his assets in just a single day, and triple them within a month. The business was soaring until the recession hit. In a short time, 70 percent of his wealth was lost; his remaining wealth is being spent on leasing installments, rents and insurance. He decided to look for a new career, which he most certainly found.

Dan offers favors to older, wealthy women—a.k.a. sugar mamas. An all-American gigolo! It isn't a personal sexual fetish—sleeping with older women—but rather, an excellent business. For this reason, he is traveling to California to visit a woman 20 years his senior. He tells me that her annual income is in the six figures and that she has requested for him to come to California to *install her kitchen*. "If I spend a few weeks *installing her kitchen*," he tells me with a wink, "I can expect to get 10,000 to 20,000 dollars. I'm pretty good at installing kitchens." He turns away with a grin.

We travel in the Mustang through New Mexico and Arizona for 10 hours until we reach Las Vegas, Nevada. The landscape is stunning; I silently take in the sight of the majestic desert and huge rock formations flashing past my window. After a few hours Dan is tired (probably more from talking than driving) and he lets me take over behind the wheel.

Driving that Mustang on Route 66 towards the sunset is one of the best experiences (and soon to be best memories) I have from this trip thus far.

Early in the evening we reach the Grand Canyon. Dan somehow has an entry pass for all national parks, so we get to enjoy the phenomenal view in the huge chasms of the canyon for free. The color of the setting sun makes the red rock formations glow. Dan and I sit beside each other in silence for the next hour admiring the view. It all feels so surreal, like a dream; when I think back to just 24 hours ago, it feels as though I have moved between two very different planets.

6/ No Gifts in the Wild West
(Las Vegas)

Everything or nothing: work in Las Vegas

Dan and I reach Las Vegas at around midnight. Prior to this I have written to numerous couch surfers in the city, almost without any success. Luckily, a woman named Elyssa agreed to my request, but according to Dan's navigation device, she lives at the other end of the city.

A woman my own age receives me when I finally arrive at Elyssa's. She lets me into the house without any words or greeting, lies down on a recliner chair, and stares at me. Sitting next to me is a young couch surfer from India who is equally unsure of Elyssa's behavior. He tries to start a conversation and break her silence by making funny faces; his attempts remain unsuccessful. She continues to stare at us, utterly expressionless.

I wonder whether Elyssa has taken drugs and is high, or if she's simply depressed. From what I can see, her apartment is a huge mess. Adding to this is the unforgiving stench coming from what can only be dirty kitty litter. I lie down with the other couch surfer on a bunk bed in Elyssa's kitchen, but can only sleep for three hours; I tiptoe out of the house at six in the morning, determined to find a hotel room for myself.

Las Vegas is a city that shouldn't be there at all. Originally it was a Christian settlement, but in 1931, the legalization of gambling in the federal state of Nevada laid down the cornerstone for the rapid growth of the desert city. In 1941, mobster Bugsy Siegel built the first hotel with a casino; today there are more than 1,000 casinos that border both Fremont Street and the Strip, each magnificently built next to one another and attracting tourists from around the world. Every year more than 30 million visitors come here, of which only five percent admit that they come only for the entertainment; that leaves 95 percent falling for the temptations offered by Sin City. Most people end up trying to score with Madame Lady Luck at one of the numerous gambling tables.

It shouldn't be too difficult to get a free room in a city full of hotels (one would think). Unfortunately, that is not the case. I start my quest at eight that morning, first at the Rio Hotel, when the temperature is still at 86 degrees Fahrenheit.

At around ten, at Excalibur, the temperature has risen to 95 degrees.

By noon, at over 105 degrees, I am politely directed to the exit of the Mirage.

Las Vegas may appear to be a happy place, but the fun is soon over if one has no dough. Many receptionists look at me with distaste, and some assume that I am homeless, a liar, or both. I am also tired and thirsty. The water taps in the hotel bathrooms provide only short-term relief; after a few minutes back in the heat, I am again as thirsty as earlier. I feel myself as being the human version of the Sea of Galilee: water flows in and nothing flows out, but the water level reduces constantly. I refill my two-liter drinking bottle about four times, which means that I have drunk about six to eight liters of water already. The highest temperature that day, even in the shade, is 110 degrees.

After about fifty rejections I decide to change my approach—sometimes with humor and sometimes more reserved—but there's still no sale. My motivation to persevere comes from the thought of having to spend another night on one of Elyssa's bunk beds; unsurprisingly, I would much rather nurse my cold by watching movies in a cozy hotel room than sleep next to the kitty litter. Hot, thirsty, but undeterred, I continue on my mission.

The casino hotels in Las Vegas belong to three big resort companies. Naturally, a floor manager cannot decide whether someone can stay overnight for free without consulting the head office first. However, because it is a Saturday, this makes it impossible because no one will be available before Monday. I remember the film *Casino* with Robert De Niro and Joe Pesci. The plot is built around the Las Vegas of the sixties and seventies, when the biggest hotels belonged to the mafia. At the end of the film, Robert De Niro, playing Sam "Ace" Rothstein, is the only one to survive the mafia war and the police. He describes how Las Vegas will change by the end of the seventies and that the resort companies will take over the role of the mafia and they will manage the hotels.

Had the mafia not been so greedy, a Robert De Niro lookalike may have been sitting in a hotel office, serving as the boss, wearing a silk suit and with a cigar stuck in his mouth. He probably would willingly offer me the presidential suite where the only catch was to be in the Mafia's debt for the rest of my life: *Sure, you can stay in the best suite. Your life just belongs to us now.* After eight hours of fruitless search, I seriously consider accepting such a deal if it is offered to me at this moment in time; I just want to go to sleep.

Another reason why it's impossible for me to find a free room is THE BIGGEST FUCKING SHOE FAIR EVER! The fair is taking place this weekend, attracting a crowd of shoe wholesalers who have filled up all the hotels. I could understand if the biggest shoe fair took place in the Thuringian Forest, or in the Spanish Way of St. James where one certainly needs a lot of shoes for trekking, but why here and why now in the desert of Nevada with temperatures of 110 degrees? Here, one needs many things, but shoes certainly can't be at the top of the list.

Despite all the obstacles, at around four-thirty in the afternoon I come to a classic west coast motel from a much earlier time. The eight-meter-long neon sign reading *TOD Motor Motel* has certainly seen better days, but the furniture in the reception area is rather stylish...for 1968. I speak to Fred, who is the manager of the motel. Without any hesitation, he says that I can have a room for a few days simply because he finds my story interesting.

This would have had a happy ending were it not for Tod, the owner of the motel. There is a Tod, and he exists, and this is his motor hotel. Fred introduces me to Tod and explains that I don't have any money. Tod, aghast, asks me if I'm going to be staying there. When I nod, he gets going: "Now *this* is a fucking story. You never travel without money!"

Tod is really pissed off. I tell him quickly and nervously about my whole trip. Tod asks, though it feels more like interrogating, specific questions to every last detail. I rattle off everything in bits and pieces: working on the container ship, Montreal and space cookies, a hundred dollar bill and a bicycle from the Amish, being homeless in Albuquerque...am I forgetting anything?

Tod looks taken aback, as if he isn't expecting such a response made up of all these unusual facts in 30 seconds. Still, he persists, claiming that I'm "a fucking scam" and asks why Fred can't see that. Fred stays relaxed and asks me to continue with my story. I pause for a moment when Dan, with his sugar mamas who finance his life, comes to my mind. I narrate in detail the story about him and the Mustang Fastback and how I drove it on Route 66, sparing no adjective in describing the magic and power of the vehicle.

Tod smiles now for the first time. He likes this story much better than that of the homeless or the Amish. "Okay, it could be true," he snarls. "But you only stay here if we make a deal first!" He offers me several nights' stay in the motel if, in exchange, I make an advertisement video for his hotel. I accept gladly and finally get to lie down on a real bed.

For the next few days I survive solely on the pancakes offered by the motel. Normally I drink tap water, but owing to the high chlorine content here, it tastes horrible, so I find a new source of hydration. On the Vegas Strip I go through the different outlets with an empty cup from McDonald's, in order to refill my drink from the McDonald's soda machines. No one really checks to see who refills the cups, so it goes rather smoothly. I am growing more and more innovative by the day.

After three days in the TOD Motor Motel, Tod thanks me for the small advertising video that I made for his motel. However, since he needs the room for paying guests, he also politely suggests that I continue on with my journey. I still haven't found any way of traveling further and haven't made any preemptive arrangements, but I have to find another place to stay.

The Rodeway Inn agrees to take me in for the nights to come. The manager, David, responds to the tale of my trip: "Oh, that's kind of cool!" And I also find it kind of cool when he promises me a three-night stay with breakfast included. This hotel also has a pool and offers higher-standard rooms compared to the TOD Motor Motel: cable TV, good air-conditioning, and two double beds. For breakfast, they offer hot cereal, cornflakes, and a variety of cakes. Even though cakes are not the healthiest choice, I manage to fill myself up with so much food that it keeps me full until well into the afternoon.

David also wants a return service for the three-night stay. He hasn't a clue as to how or when or where he will use this video, but he wants a full interview with himself and he wants to do it with both of my cameras set up. Naturally, I can and will do this for him. On that same day, I set up both the cameras in the entry area of Rodeway Inn: one camera will be on the tripod and the other, with a super wide-angle lens and a microphone attached to it, will be held by hand. I even see to it that the microphone also has one of those fluffy windsocks on it so that everything looks professional.

The interview lasts for about 30 minutes and David speaks about his career as the manager for the Rodeway Inn, starting from when he first arrived from the East Coast and applied for the manager position. He adds that, since then, the Rodeway Inn has expanded by so many rooms, but that the pool is still the same as it was eleven years ago. I ask him about the guests. He tells me that many are very young, often college students, but that there are also older guests who come in the fall to visit the numerous fairs. This is then followed by the story of the new paved roads in front of the hotel; he muses that it must have been unbelievably hot for the road workers while tarring in the desert heat.

We also talk about the many drunken tourists in the city, which are not at all that bad. I ask him about his favorite city, his greatest desires in life, and also how it feels to live in a desert. He answers that there are many beautiful cities in the world, including New York and San Francisco, but that European cities are also very beautiful.

We then talk about his expectations; for example, a salary raise, or a certain type of guest. He informs me that the desert around Las Vegas is not at all that bad, and apart from the months of June to August, the climate is excellent. I again think of the film *Casino* and the countless wise guys buried in the desert. David then talks about bowling: a wonderful sport. Twice a week he meets his friends for bowling, but lately many of them have been quite irregular for the training.

After the interview David and I shake hands with respect, because we have completed a fair deal in which both of us have gained something. David is satisfied with his interview, and I with the hotel for three nights. The following day I set out to organize my trip; after all, I do want to reach Antarctica at some point. In this 110-degree heat, it is a destination that seems too far away. Now that I know hitchhiking doesn't really work here, I have to somehow earn some money for my journey ahead. As I stand in front of Bellagio, one of the biggest hotels in the city, I can't help but be distracted with a spectacular water show that takes place every hour between the hotel and the street.

This seems to be the perfect place for introducing the *human sofa*. Since there are a lot of tourists here and it's over 104 degrees Fahrenheit, no one is really walking…it's more like crawling. I ingeniously find my niche market: I will offer the overheated and tired tourist a place to take a seat and rest. I stand with a large cardboard sign in front of a water fountain: *A human sofa for one dollar! Anyone can sit and relax on my back for just one dollar.*

At first none of the tourists understand what I am offering because they don't see a sofa anywhere, so I decide to make my human sofa concept more apparent by going down on all four limbs. I put a white pillow on my back so that the human sofa can also offer a little more comfort. My cardboard sign hangs from my neck and dangles before me on the pavement. The passersby now understand my offer and they laugh, chuckle, and even cheer for the human sofa. Just when my first customer takes a seat on me, the security guards of the Bellagio interfere in my business and indicate that the pavement also happens to be the property of the hotel and I must get off of it.

I move further away, nearer to the bus stop, and kneel down on all fours posing as a human sofa again. Business is getting busier as families all want to take turns and relax on my back. There is hustle and bustle all around me; people distributing flyers or selling concert tickets. I decide that I need to look for a new spot for the human sofa, far away from the security guards and the street hawkers, so I enter St. Mark's Square, which is modeled after the one in Italy: it even has a replica of Campanile von San Marco in its center.

The church tower here is the entrance to Madame Tussaud's Wax Museum. Hordes of people come in through the tower on the moving walkways. The perfect spot for the human sofa! I kneel down again and this time it draws in even more people who see me from afar. I call out again and again, "Human sofa, take a seat for just one dollar! Special price! Just one dollar for the human sofa!" People are enthusiastic and a few actually take a seat. A group of extremely drunk college students comes along. One of the guys feels like he must (and wants to) help me, so he starts shouting over the moving walkways: "Haaaave a seat on thiiiiis huuuuuuuman soooooofa!" The people feel rather intimidated now, thinking that the drunken guy is with me; nobody dares to take a seat. I call it a day and count my earnings. In total, only seven dollars, but I am still proud.

With this loot I go to Circus Circus, which is one of the casino hotels on the Strip that attracts people with neon signs, roller coasters, and extremely loud music. I exchange five of my seven dollars in the casino for a chip. There is a free introductory course here for blackjack, so I attend. Actually, blackjack is very easy if one knows the game—the aim is to get as close to 21 points as possible with the cards, without going bust. If one does not go beyond 21 points and has more points than the dealer, then one wins a round and doubles his money.

I decide to let it all ride on my five-dollar chip. Both of my cards tally up to eleven points, so I draw one more card. It's a seven—safe! A total of eighteen points, not bad. The dealer draws a card and shows his hand: nineteen points. My money is gone.

Feeling quite frustrated, I spot a big old man sitting at one of the poker tables with heaps of chips in front of him (which must equal around 3,000 dollars, at least). With his XXL T-shirt, shorts, and old gym shoes, he doesn't appear to be very wealthy. Within a few minutes his heap of chip halves. Intrigued, I go to talk with him, and he introduces himself as Sam. But Sam doesn't want to talk about himself or his passion for gambling; he finds my trip without money more interesting. He calls his buddy over, a fellow named Roy Cooke, and briefly shares my story with him, then invites me to his house, which turns out to be in one of the so-called gated areas, i.e. a fenced-off area for the rich.

His friend Roy is a stout man, around 50 years old, with a mustache that makes him look like a snuggly teddy bear. He tells me that he has worked as a professional gambler for 15 years, which has made him quite rich. He doesn't want to mention the exact numbers, but I'm sure he has certainly made over five million dollars easily. I am excited to learn that one can be a professional gambler by trade and actually win money (in direct contrast to my awkward attempt today). Roy tells me that in his earlier days he had been a misfit in school, a guy who was teased by everyone. His father was a professional chess player and had introduced him to the game quite early on. During college, he noticed that he could make a lot of money with it. He quickly progressed and became a famous personality in Las Vegas. Eventually, he married a beautiful woman and started a family. I am touched by this story's lovely development.

I ask Roy whether money has made him happy. He replies quite differently from Dan or Joseph: "Yes, money has made me a much happier person!" Thanks to his riches, he has now become someone with whom one would like to be photographed with in Las Vegas. He says he is gifted, or something of an exceptional talent; someone who is extremely good at something. In his case, it's gambling. Five years ago, he decided to start a new career as a real estate agent. At first everything went well and he could almost double his five million with his lands and houses, but then came the economic crisis, and now *90 percent* of his assets are gone; he faces total ruin.

I am shocked that this unbelievable story unfolds without a Hollywood ending. He became rich through gambling, and lost almost everything by working. How Roy can sit there, totally relaxed and without bitterness, continues to bewilder me to this day. Before I take leave of him, he gives me a useful tip for the rest of my journey: "Shut up and deal!" He grins and closes the door.

The next morning I stand at the exit ramp of Freeway 15 with two dollars in my pocket and a big cardboard sign with the letters *LA* on it. I assume that almost every semiliterate adult all over the world can interpret these two letters as an abbreviation for one of the greatest metropolitan cities in the United States; however, a middle-aged woman stops. No, she doesn't want to take me along, but instead is only curious to know what the two letters on the signboard are supposed to mean. She doesn't see LA as *L and A*, (two separate letters) but instead as the word *"la"*, and asks me what my sign is trying to say. I am, for one of the only times I can recall, speechless.

7/ Everybody Has a Dream (Los Angeles)

Wayne, who finally takes pity on me on the Las Vegas roads, drops me off on the outskirts of Los Angeles. I feel lucky because soon afterwards, I get to know Fred at the nearest gas station and he offers to take me along. "I just need to do something quickly," he tells me. So I watch him as he drives his huge pick-up truck to the parking lot by the gas station and meets a young woman there. They kiss and there is continuous hugging, again and again. In this vein, the short meeting becomes a two-hour affair, and I occasionally glance over at them as I attempt to amuse myself with my thoughts. Finally, my patience pays off when Fred (who is in a really good mood) offers to take me along to Santa Monica, where I have received an invitation from a couch surfer named James.

Fred is in his mid-40s and looks like a cross between Danny DeVito and Dirk Bach, the rotund German television comedian. As we drive through the endless sea of houses in Los Angeles, he tells me about the details of his relationship and that for the first time in his life he is ready to move away from the coast for a woman. They have already made plans for their future together.

"She is the most wonderful woman in the world," he keeps repeating. "This is the real thing. Do you know what I mean? *The real thing.*" I am impressed with his strong love and ask how long they have known each other.

"Eight days, man. Today was our second date."

In Santa Monica, James receives me in an elegant apartment near the beach. He truly appears to be the Los Angeles cliché: he is 34 years old, very good-looking, and has three jobs—all of which are somehow connected to Hollywood. His main job and source of income is as a masseuse for Hollywood celebrities. Every now and then, he tells me, a good-looking masseuse connects with famous Hollywood actresses, sometimes offering a little extra *relaxation*. He recently completed a course in Thai massage, and says that by adding a few Thai words here and there during a massage, he can heighten the overall experience and bump up business.

His second job is as a scriptwriter for various television shows and films. I conclude that James is probably the typical *Starbucks writer*—a writer without much success who sits in front of his MacBook every day (any other laptop would be completely unacceptable) and writes the next big blockbuster. The Oscar for *Best Poser in Screenwriting* will certainly 100 percent go to him—emphasis being on the poser bit.

The third job is obvious: he is, unfailingly, an actor.

James also talks about some smaller jobs: he works as a DJ in a small bar, and also regularly sends out his modeling photos. With a moderate record of success, he doesn't give up. At some point in time he will live the all-American dream and make it big in Hollywood—or at least he hopes to.

On the first night, James tells me a lot about his life: about how he left the countryside in order to make a career here in Hollywood, about how he believes in himself and that anything is possible, and about how cool it is to be part of the glamorous Hollywood life. During our one-sided conversation (James is more of a talker than a listener) he keeps glancing at the large mirror in the living room and moves his hand through his hair. He asks me whether he is good-looking. Naturally I say yes, and for a flourish, add, "You look like the Swiss singer Patrick Nuo. He is known for his good looks."

James likes this: a resemblance to a European celebrity sounds great. He asks me what women like the most about Patrick Nuo: is it his eyes? His mouth? His body? Then he takes his shirt off, shows me the muscles he's been training for, and asks if I can clearly see them; then, whether or not his hair is too long. The questions about him are never-ending, and at some point I just doze off.

The next morning James takes me to the Santa Monica airport. The small airport mainly serves rich business people hopping from one meeting to the next in their private jets. In front of the terminal I am tempted to present myself as an air-hitchhiker, as just maybe there is a businessman or woman who is heading to South America for a meeting and wouldn't mind taking along some company or a personal butler. Thinking it a brilliant idea, I change into my butler uniform in order to increase my chances.

About 500 aircraft take off and land every day at this airport. I ask the clerk at the information counter whether any more flights are planned for the day. She replies in a reserved, severe way, requesting that I leave the premises immediately. In front of the building I ask the passengers how one can hitchhike with a private jet, but no one wants to help me.

Disappointed, I wander through the endless streets of Los Angeles. It's not because of my butler attire that I raise suspicion with the locals; it's the fact that I am walking and not driving. All Angelenos seem to have cars. If you do not believe this, just take look at one of the overcrowded freeways: the City of Angels is a city of cars. Although there is a local public transport system, only a few residents seem aware that a fully functional subway exists.

Los Angeles is simply not made for pedestrians. The city is much too spread out to reach any destination by foot. If you want to visit friends or go to the movies, you have to travel long stretches. For instance, it takes almost an hour to get from Hollywood to Santa Monica by car (provided that there are no traffic jams). Above this reality, Hollywood actually tries to promote greener lifestyles; stars like Leonardo Di Caprio, Cameron Diaz or Justin Timberlake all buy hybrid cars. But you have to wonder if, secretly, they miss their Porsches and Hummers.

After walking for a few miles, a patrol car stops behind me. A cop steps out and says that some of the staff from the airport has filed a complaint against me. I assume that my journey-to-the-end-of-the-world-without-money story won't be met with much interest here, so I tell him that I am a German tourist and was asking about flights to Mexico. He asks for my passport. I rummage through my bag, but I can't find it. As I search deeper, I notice that the cop doesn't take his eyes off my hands. I struggle even more with my bag and he takes two steps back, observing me carefully with his right hand on his gun. I try to lighten the situation with a few stereotypical jokes about the German tourists in Los Angeles, but he continues to remain serious.

I find the document and swiftly hand it over. After examining my passport, the police officer scans me from top to bottom. There is an uncomfortable silence between us until he asks me whether I always wander around dressed like this. I look down and I realize that I am still dressed as a butler. Shaking his head, he gives me back my passport and goes away with the request to "clarify the thing with the flight as soon as possible". Phew. I can breathe again.

I change my clothes behind a KFC restaurant and carry on. People I ask during my walk tell me that the Los Angeles International Airport is just around the corner. After walking for almost three hours and around 400 corners, I finally reach it. I enter the terminal and begin asking the ticket counters of United Airlines, Delta, Continental, and American Airlines for a free air ticket to Mexico. The employees of the airlines refuse, saying that such matters have to be clarified in writing with the central offices, which happen to be elsewhere in Chicago, New York and Seattle.

Exhausted and frustrated, I follow the sea of houses back to James. I tell him about my day while James listens and nods sympathetically. However, in the next breath he asks when I will actually continue on with my journey. Hint taken: I have overstayed my welcome. In the late afternoon I find free Wi-Fi down the street and log onto the internet to search for a ride to San Francisco. The city is not actually on my route to Antarctica, but I know a German couple living there who, before I started my trip, had offered to take me in if I happened to pass through. A small detour to visit them is exactly what I need.

Now I need to earn some money for my ride, so I head down to the Santa Monica beach. In desperation, only one idea pops into my mind: I will go around with a tube of sunscreen and offer to apply it onto people's backs for just one dollar. I must admit that even I find this a little creepy, but I forge ahead regardless.

The majority of men find my concept to be intrusive and wrong. Who would want another man rubbing cream all over them? It isn't that kind of beach. The women are even more repulsed—not only is this strange man offering to rub cream all over their backs, but he is also charging them a dollar for it. I have to change my tactics. Instead of a complete sun-creaming session, I now offer people the opposite: for one dollar, not only will I not touch them, but I will also not bother them again.

This offer works much better. Within two hours I am able to make 13 dollars, which brings me a step closer to San Francisco. I go back to the Wi-Fi corner at Santa Monica Boulevard and check my e-mail, where I find that a woman has written back to me, offering to take me to San Francisco the next day for 35 dollars.

When I arrive back to James's place, his roommate opens the door for me. I tell her about my situation, and how, before tomorrow morning, I need to make another 22 dollars in order to pay for my ride to San Francisco. She nods, grabs her purse, and puts the money in my hand. I can't decide whether she is just being extremely generous, or if she just wants me out of the flat. Nonetheless, I am off to San Francisco in the morning.

8/ Advanced Pillow Fighting (San Francisco)

Campsite with a view: San Francisco

The next morning I travel north with Sarah, who responded to my query on the internet. Interstate 405 is the busiest interstate of the U.S. and runs from San Diego to San Fernando. Sarah is very familiar with this route, and flies down the interstate despite the speed limits. She is in her mid-twenties, has Vietnamese parents, and works as accountant in Los Angeles. For weeks she has been attempting to retrieve a parcel from Vietnam that is stuck in the central post office of San Francisco for inexplicable reasons. Sarah is trying again today for the third time to pick up her parcel. Like her previous two trips, she rents a car and looks for a fellow passenger to minimize the travel cost. In the last two trips she was turned away by the post office with the argument that the responsible person was not available. However, she is convinced that this time it will be different.

Six hours later, she parks the car at the post office in San Francisco, directly in front of the *No Stopping* sign, and requests that I wait for her. She hurries into the building as I sit in the passenger seat. Shortly thereafter, she comes back. There is still no trace of her parcel. Disheartened, we part ways, and she returns to Los Angeles.

When I reach Thomas and Kathrin, my German friends, there is a surprise waiting for me: my very own parcel from home that a good friend sent to this address. The parcel contains whole-grain bread, cereal bars, sweets, spreads, a package of sauerkraut, shower gel, and much more. I have never been so happy to receive such a package. While I am arranging my new treasures in front of me, Kathrin and Thomas talk about their life here in America, which they moved to a year ago. Thomas is a computer scientist and is looking forward to a career in the Silicon Valley, not very far from San Francisco. They share a spacious apartment in Haight-Ashbury, the famous neighborhood where the hippie culture originated in the sixties.

We speak in German, eat German treats, and watch the *Tagesschau* (German daily news) over the course of the night. Sitting on the sofa with a woolen blanket over my legs, I feel like I am at home in Berlin. Since my package provides some reserves for the next few days, the next morning I take a tour of the city.

It is, so far, the highlight of my trip. Architecturally, San Francisco can probably compete with any European city. Every house is an original; no two are alike. Because San Francisco is at constant risk of earthquakes, large parts of its buildings are made of wood. San Francisco is also known for its Victorian-styled homes that were built during the Gold Rush era in the middle of the 19th century. Although many houses became victims of the earthquake and the fire of 1906, there are still about 15,000 Victorian structures existing in the city today.

There are also some buildings here, quite old ones, which you don't see too often in the United States. The Mission Dolores Church, for instance, is really a magnificent building that was built by the Spaniards in

1776. Contrasting this is the downtown core, which comes across like a smaller version of New York. I run through the deep street canyons that were built in the various decades of the 20th century, and gaze up at The Transamerica Pyramid, probably the most well-known landmark in the downtown area. My tour takes up the whole day, from the Golden Gate Bridge to zigzag Lombard Street, and I even ride on the cable cars up the steep hills. It is mild and sunny; the weather this city is known for.

I am blown away by San Francisco and would like to stay here forever. However, time is pressing. It is now the middle of August and if I really want to make it to Antarctica, I must reach Ushuaia—the most southern city of Tierra del Fuego—by the 7th of November.

Before and during the trip, I send out e-mails to research companies, scientists, and tour operators who can register me as a worker on a ship. Many of them do not respond, or simply refuse, but eventually a Chilean shipping company agrees to my request. In their e-mail, they tell me that I can travel with their ship to Antarctica if I can work on board and take the first ship of the season on the 7th of November. Apparently, during that time there aren't so many tourists on board. Since there is no choosing the ship's sail date, I stake everything on reaching Ushuaia in twelve weeks and plan out my next few days in detail.

Every morning I get up at seven. From nine to twelve, I go to a different part of the city each day to collect food from the shops. This way I can see more of the city and also avoid making the mistake of asking the same shop twice for donations. So within ten days, I visit the artsy and alternative Mission District, the colorful and gay Castro District, Union Square (where the men wear suits), and the vibrant Haight-Ashbury neighborhood with its organic markets for hippies, eco-activists and health fanatics. Every morning I manage to collect enough food to feed myself for the whole day.

The plan for each afternoon is to earn money, as I need an air ticket to Central America. Only with an ambitious leap over Mexico, Nicaragua, Honduras, El Salvador, Belize, and Guatemala, and finally over to Costa Rica, will I be able to make it on time to board the Chilean ship to Antarctica. Moreover, it currently isn't the safest time to travel to these countries alone and without money: in Mexico, the crime rate linked to the drug trade has recently soared. In Honduras, a military coup has taken place within the last month. I need to find money to reach Costa Rica, but how?

I can't offer any talent for the street arts. I can't sing or paint or do pantomime (as I love the art of talking too much). So what can I offer? On the first day I sell myself as a "hill helper". I paint my offer on a big cardboard and hang it around my neck: *Hill Helper for just one dollar!* I go and stand at one of the extreme slopes in San Francisco:

the world famous Lombard Street, which Steve McQueen hurtles down in the film *Bullitt*.

This appears to be the best spot, because the incline here is a whopping 27 percent. The tourists laugh and find my service offer interesting indeed. However, there is just one problem: the hill helper is required to support the customer with his hands in order to push the groaning customer up the hill. For many tourists, this may be too close of contact with a complete stranger. Many give me a thumbs-up for the good idea, but make it up the hill on their own. However, there are some who do take me up on my offer, and I push some Brits, French, and Germans up the steep hill. Depending upon their comfort level, they are allowed to lean back and rest their entire weight onto me. Each dollar earned is a real backbreaking experience (almost literally), as some of the tourists exceed 200 pounds. At the end of the day I have collected 30 dollars.

On the second afternoon, I have another idea. In Berlin, I once participated in a huge pillow fight in the trendy pub Bar 25. It was incredible to see how the cool Berliners suddenly shed all their inhibitions and participated in this childish game of striking each other upside the head with huge pillows. Would this work with…Americans?

In Thomas and Kathrin's kitchen I make a huge cardboard sign saying *Pillow fight me for just one dollar!* that covers two-thirds of my body. They both lend me their pillows—at least this way they will get nicely fluffed-up.

Kathrin suggests that I try going to Fisherman's Wharf, one of the biggest tourist spots in the city. Upon my arrival I can see that the sidewalk where the street artists are permitted is about 100 feet long. Standing on one side are the hip-hoppers, pantomimes, and spray painters, while on the other are the beggars with signs saying *Please money for weed! Please money for beer!*

The new guy holding two pillows causes a chuckle amongst most of the street artists, what with my unusual idea, but no one is welcoming the competition. However, the passersby are coming up to me and saying either "Pillow fighting for a buck? That is so cool!" or "Man, you're funny, just take two dollars!" Many tourists seem to love my idea. A class of junior high kids takes turns. When the group finishes, completely out of breath, one of the students puts a five-dollar bill in my moneybox and says, in absolute seriousness, "One day I want to be like you." Often groups of men walk by, and when one man strays slightly from his group, I take the opportunity to attack him with my pillow for a quick dollar. Whenever there is a fight, many people stop to watch, cheer, and share the fun.

Later in the afternoon, two men in suits want to fight with each other, and I find it quite amusing to earn two dollars without having to fight either of them myself. Both of them strike each other with pillows as if they have some unsettled score to settle. The bigger of the two falls down after missing a blow, and is properly strangled by his adversary with his pillow. He lies like a tortoise on his back, struggling to get onto his feet, and finally succeeds in freeing himself from his opponent with a kick. I laugh out loud, wondering what I have started. The next day I decide to take the fight to Golden Gate Park, which resembles Central Park in New York in both its dimensions and landscape architecture.

After 45 pillow fights, I am 68 dollars closer to my goal. A group of college students makes me 18 dollars in one go; during this battle, instantly, the innocent pillow fight becomes a matter of patriotism between Germany and the U.S. It is the Olympics, only Wigge-style. I have to compete five times with different athletes representing the U.S. The rest of the group is cheering, of course, for the American competitors, chanting "U-S-A, U-S-A!"

During an intensive pillow fight with one of the girls, one of the students shouts out: "Hit him for the bad Audi the Germans have sold me!"

The rest of the group laughs and another student adds, "Hit him also for the VW Fahrvergnügen!" Some years ago, Volkswagen had run a very successful advertising campaign in the U.S. in which the German word *Fahrvergnügen* was introduced into the English language. The word even acquired a cult status in the United States; as a result, stickers with similar sounding phrases, like *fuck the fuel,* are sold across the country.

For this reason, the rest of the group seizes this phrase vociferously: "Yes, the Fahrvergnügen was bad. Hit him for that fuckin' Fahrvergnügen!"

Another student adds: "And the Germans love David Hasselhoff! Punch him for that!" It continues like this for a while, and I get further blows with the pillows for German sausages, Boris Becker, and Schumacher's Formula One successes.

The following day, I fight 40 more pillow fights for 50 dollars in a small downtown park. Many professionals manage to squeeze in a small pillow fight between their work duties, lunches, and business meetings. On this day I meet Justin, who is 23 years old and originally from Florida. Over the past six months he has been traveling across the country, and for the last two months now he has been living voluntarily homeless here in downtown San Francisco. He is fascinated by my pillow fights and plans to organize his trip in a similar fashion to mine; he also finds my ideas for pillow fighting, the human sofa, and the hill helper much cooler than simply begging.

Justin tells me that he left his old existence in search of the true purpose of life. In the meantime, he has also realized that homelessness and begging do nothing to help him develop spiritually. He now puts everything into the pillow fights. I wish him the best of luck and I'm happy to have inspired him. The next day, Monday, it is slightly rainy and I earn only 15 dollars; but when it clears up later in the afternoon I make another 40 dollars over 30 pillow fights in Dolores Park.

With each fight I become more of a pillow fight expert, and by the end of my stay in San Francisco, I can even differentiate between different pillow fighting techniques:

Windmill: the fighter holds the pillow in the right hand and rotates the arm like the sail of a windmill. This rotation makes for a very dangerous pillow-fighting technique.

Sword fight: although no swords are used here, the pillow is moved towards the adversary in the classical sword fight position by thrusting it at the opponent in a diagonal slice from top left to bottom right, and from top right to bottom left.

Shot put: in this technique, one jabs the pillow directly into the face of the adversary; no swinging, no wrestling, and no rotating, simply straight in. This technique is simple, but very effective, as I come to know every time I get struck and fall to the ground.

Deceive: this one is frequently used in Dolores Park. The opponent tricks you by starting with one technique, but changing fight strategy at the very last second. The attack is then mostly made with a horizontal rotational movement (known as the *Propeller*).

Strangling: as the name already implies, the person using *Strangling* waits for the opportunity to gag her adversary properly with the pillow after making him fall to the ground through the *Deceive*. Women like to use this technique.

After nearly 250 fights, I have finally collected 300 dollars. I start looking for cheap one-way tickets to Costa Rica on the internet. All the flights cost between 400 and 500 dollars, with one significant exception: I find a flight on the 11th of September for a little less than 300 dollars. The Americans are still recovering from the 2001 tragedy and many just choose not to fly on this date, so the airline companies drop their prices in hopes of once again attracting passengers. I go ahead and book my flight for the 11th of September, but what am I going to do for the next two weeks?

By chance I meet Bryan and Murph, two Americans in their mid-30s, during a particularly intense round of pillow fighting. Both of them live one hour away from San Francisco in Vacaville (which translates to *"one-cow town")*, which probably explains their interest in my crazy stories. I tell them that I have two weeks to kill and ask for some suggestions. They offer to buy me a flight ticket to anywhere in the USA if I do something crazy for them.

Anywhere? Hawaii! This may be my only chance to see it on this trip. We look at airfares, and the flights are between 400 and 450 dollars. This is quite expensive fun for the both of them, and so they would like to see something special. Bryan suggests that I should run naked with pink angel wings across the Golden Gate Bridge while they film it. I would consider this trade-off fair if there were no YouTube, or internet in general. We go over different ideas of what I can do for the air ticket. The ideas that emerge become more and more obtuse, and at some point I give up on the idea of going to Hawaii.

The next day I meet up with Murph again, and he is ecstatic. He has spoken to his father, who was a pilot for United Airlines for 25 years, and as a benefit he can still get standby tickets. These are air tickets with which one can fly for minimal cost, or even for free. The risk, however, is that one could wait for hours—or even days—at the airport for an available seat. In many cases, if you are lucky enough to be put into first class, the airline can demand a special dress code. But it seems I don't have to wait: Murph tells me, beaming with joy, that he has gotten a ticket for me to Honolulu which departs tomorrow morning. I can hardly believe this news and my luck.

How very often I have dreamed about going to Hawaii. Even if it is far from Antarctica, Hawaii it is for me.

9/ No Trouble in Paradise (Hawaii)

The early bird catches the worm: Waikiki Beach, Hawaii

At first glance, Hawaii looks exactly how the travel brochures promise. Honolulu is the capital city of Hawaii and has almost 400,000 inhabitants. At the famous Waikiki beach, tourists can literally walk from their hotel rooms and straight onto the beach within mere minutes. The warm sand and the crystal blue water, together with the mountainous backdrop covered in tropical greenery, truly make Hawaii a paradise. This group of islands is named the Sandwich Islands in honor of John Montagu IV, the Earl of Sandwich, who financed the expedition of the islands by British explorer James Cook.

I'm again couch surfing, spending the first two nights at Martin's. Martin lives with his girlfriend in a very small and overpriced apartment. The housing prices are very expensive in Hawaii for one simple reason: everyone wants to live here on an island where land is limited. During the day I wander around the center of Honolulu, and conclude that the Hawaiian mentality seems really relaxed. This makes the popular *shaka* hand gesture, which means *hang loose*, a more fitting greeting than the typical wave. Wherever I ask, everyone seems to have an extra apple or banana they can spare to a hungry tourist. With this experience in mind, I decide to check out one of the most happening restaurants on Waikiki beach.

I approach the manager of the restaurant and, in a very polite and respectful tone, ask if he has anything he could offer me to eat since I don't have any money and I'm trying to travel to the end of the world. He takes some time to think before he responds that he's sure they must have something. He likes my travel story and invites me to take a seat and order what I like. I am ecstatic and in awe at how easy it is. I sit down at one of the nicest tables and order the steak with a side of vegetables, as it has been several weeks since I have had any vegetables. As I am waiting for my meal, I take a look around and notice that all of the customers are smartly-dressed, while I am in a pair of dirty shorts and flip-flops.

Later on, the manager, Sam, takes a seat at my table and explains why he had said yes to my request: "I like people who go travel and see the world. It's important to open our minds to other cultures so that we can be more tolerant and stop the prejudice against other races." Realizing that I couldn't have put it any better myself, I sink my teeth into my big, juicy steak. I can hardly believe that I am getting this delicious 48-dollar meal for free.

Later I head to the North Shore, where Victor, a 28-year old couch surfer, has agreed to take me in. For most of the year, the waves here are perfect. This reason alone is why Victor has moved to Hawaii. Surfing, also known as the *sport of the kings*, is the most popular sport in Hawaii, though it was once reserved only for the royals. Gracing the water was considered a form of mystical meditation by the monarchs who were worshipped as gods back then. Today, of course, surfing is much more liberated: the North Shore is a surfer's paradise and it holds the famous Triple Crown of Surfing competition every year.

Besides being a passionate surfer, Victor also works in a camp for the disabled that is operated by the Salvation Army. I join him and the other staff for lunch that day. At the table, the topic of interest seems to be a naked man that been spotted on the beach. Instead of giggles and giddy comments, everyone (even the surfers) seems to be disturbed by it. I make a mental note to myself: *remember to wear swimming trunks when going to the beach.*

Feeling inspired, I tell Victor that I would like to give surfing a try—or at least, have him take some cool photos of me on a surfboard. He gives me a hesitant look but then agrees, and early the next morning we head to the beach with a couple of surfboards. With a lot of patience, Victor shows and explains how one should stand on a surfboard. I practice again and again on the sand until I get it. Now into the water! My rhythm seems to be slip, flip and fall; I haven't managed to pull myself up on the board yet. Victor just laughs and encourages me to keep at it. A little while later, he discreetly leaves me alone with my board and goes out further into the waves with the other surfers.

I continue to try on my own but this process doesn't see any improvements, other than adding "gasping", "crawling", and "hanging on" to my overall rhythm. Finally, I manage to catch a wave and ride it standing rather than all of the other positions I was doing. What a feeling! Although I quickly fall down again, I paddle back out and start all over again while wearing a satisfied grin. The other surfers watch me as I make my best attempt at their sport. They probably have never seen such an embarrassment before. One of them actually comes up to me and asks me whether I am shooting a comedy and if that is the reason why I am surfing the way I am. I politely reply no, and explain that I simply cannot surf. Natalie, a friend of Victor's who is also there surfing, observes my unique surfing style and comes over to say, only half-jokingly, "That is the weirdest thing I have ever seen!" With that, my future surfing career comes to a premature end.

Anyways, I have other things to do: my clothes have become quite dirty during this trip. With the ocean right here, it's a good time to give my trousers, T-shirt, underpants and socks a good scrub. I can see Victor shaking his head from a distance as he tries to take the next wave. A surfer passes by me as I am scrubbing and sarcastically remarks, "I didn't know that the North Shore was a part of India!"

After the washing, I notice that one of my socks is pretty ruined. Since I have only the one pair on me, I'll have to manage without it. Washing clothes has been a constant challenge throughout this entire trip: after the nice Amish couple had washed my clothes, the next opportunity was the bathtub in my hotel room in Las Vegas. When I had reached San Francisco, I had hoped to wash my clothes at Kathrin and Thomas's place, but—just my luck—their washing machine wasn't working. So this washing is long, long overdue.

Now that my clothes are clean, I have another task. A few days ago, I lost my toothbrush. I was staying with Martin at the time, and I was so desperate that I secretly used his toothbrush. Not wanting to do anything like that again, I spend the rest of the day wandering through the district of Waialua asking for a free new toothbrush. Most of the people I approach don't even know how to take my story and just walk away from me. After three hours of random encounters, I spot the only supermarket in the city. I go in and give the cashier my spiel, and she directs me to the department head, who in turn sends me to the marketing manager. Understanding my money situation, he tries to sell me the most economical toothbrush the store carries.

During my earlier encounters on the street, prior to coming into the supermarket, one lone person had shown pity on me and had given me a dollar towards a toothbrush. The cheapest one that the manager can offer me is for $1.79, but, even after he generously gives me the employee discount, my dollar is still not enough. We stand there for a while; he then remembers something and goes into his office. Rummaging through his bag, he pulls out a brand-new toothbrush. He tells me that he was at the dentist earlier in the week and that he was given a new toothbrush, which I'm told is a normal procedure for dentists in the U.S. I happily leave the supermarket with my new gift.

All the different districts on the island can easily be covered by bus. One can see the entire island for just

$2.25. Of course, I don't have this fare, so I discreetly slip onto the bus without the driver noticing. I travel to meet Cassandra and her 11-year-old daughter Odessa, who live on the East Coast and have offered to put me up for a couple of nights. They live in a small house on the beach, and to me, the whole scene looks like something out of a movie: tall palm trees shading parts of the white sand beach, the sound of water splashing up against the rocks, and even the view behind the house is a huge hill covered in forest. Adding to this scene, Cassandra is sitting in her garden playing the ukulele. It's all very…Hawaii!

That evening, despite my best efforts to wash my clothes, Odessa asks her mother, "Why is he so smelly?" Cassandra is completely embarrassed and quickly explains that Odessa says this about everyone. However, I fear that Odessa is right; the smell can no longer be ignored. After washing my clothes in Las Vegas and at the North Shore, I didn't have enough time to let them dry out completely — so now they are reeking.

I go back to Martin's place to spend my last day on Oahu. He asks me to help him move into a new apartment, for which he will repay me with a plane ticket to the largest of the Hawaiian Islands, Big Island. Compared to the tiny place he was in before, the new place is literally a huge improvement and all for the same amount of rent. While we are carrying his sofa to the new apartment, he tells me that he moved here from Boston 15 years ago in order to fulfill his fantasy of living under the palm trees. He is happy to have done it, but it was a big trade-off: his job is unchallenging, doesn't pay well and he only has ten vacation days each year. This is normal here in Hawaii; with the high cost of living and the competition, you really can't be too picky. However, he concludes that if this is what it takes to live in paradise, then it's still worth it.

With the move, Martin is up to his ears in work, so I have to find another place to spend the night. Another couch surfer named Noora has agreed to take me in, and we arrange to meet at a garden party between the street canyons of Honolulu. The garden belongs to a 30-story apartment complex near the beach. When I arrive, there are 40 people are grilling, drinking, and dancing. Unfortunately, Noora doesn't turn up. Feeling a little unnerved, I start to ask some of the party guests if they have a place for me. Many of them are thrilled about my story, but none of them have a couch available. With no other options, I set up camp at Waikiki Beach. Along with the Copacabana in Rio, it's one of the most famous beaches in the world, so it's really not so bad.

Many tourists are enjoying the starry night with a walk along the beach as I pitch my tent and call it a day. At midnight, I am woken by a group of drunken people in their mid-twenties. While yelling, laughing, and doing silly stunts off the wall directly behind me, a guy's foot lands on my tent. I unzip the entrance to see what's going on. The guy, who is about three feet away from me, looks back at me and we give each other the *shaka* hand signal before he staggers off. I go back to sleep, only to be woken again at 2:00 in the morning by a deafening noise. Startled,

I jump out of my tent and wave my arms to draw attention to myself, but am blinded by three huge headlights. This enormous, noisy thing stops and veers to the left about six feet in front of me. I gradually make out that this monster is a huge tractor, pulling cleaning mats for the beach behind it. In the driver's seat I can see a man laughing. I'm so glad that, at the very least, someone found it amusing that I nearly crapped my pants. I make it to the morning with no other interruptions, but discover that my MP3 player and earphones were stolen while I was asleep.

Flying in a propeller-driven plane over the island of Maui to the eastern coast of Big Island helps me take my mind off the morning's events. Big Island is the largest, highest, and youngest of all the Hawaiian Islands—its tallest mountain, Mauna Kea, stands over 14,000 feet high. Even during winter, when it's covered with snow, the volcanoes still spit out lava every day; it flows into the sea and makes the island continuously grow.

The public transportation system on the Big Island, the Hele-On Bus, connects all of the main areas like Hilo, Kona, the volcanoes, beaches and other areas—and it's free. I am curious to know why this is so, and am given various reasons by my fellow passengers: the inhabitants of the island rely on it because they are poor and have no money to own a car; there have been too many problems with hitchhiking—with a few hitchhikers having disappeared—and this encourages less hitchhiking; the system is so convenient and connects all of the tourist sites so that it will attract even more tourists to this island. They all sound like good reasons to me, but I'm just happy to know I don't have to pay a thing to use it.

We land in the city of Hilo (population of 40,000) in the eastern part of the island. Since the clouds come in from the east, the rain falls in front of Hilo's mountain slopes. It rains 277 days out of the year here, making it the city with the highest precipitation rate in the U.S.

I had been warned before coming here that I should be careful, that there are frequent conflicts between the native inhabitants and the white people who migrated here. It dates back, as all things do, to simple history: the natives here are called *Kanaka Maoli* and they are now a minority in their own country. The Kanaka Maoli believe that the decline of the Hawaiian culture started when the British discovered this group of islands in 1778; these intruders quickly started exploiting the islands and their resources in the name of the British Crown.

In the 19th century, the Americans arrived and used Hawaii as their chief base for all of their trading business in the Pacific. In 1893, Queen Liliuokalani set out to give her country a new constitution that gave more power to the royal court. The American traders saw this as a threat to their business and decided to overthrow the queen with the help of the U.S. Navy. Since then, the U.S. military has been present here (as one knows from Pearl Harbor). Ultimately, in 1959, Hawaii became an official American state, becoming the only one in the country that had a real royal palace. The Kanaka Maoli, meanwhile, are present today at—sadly—the lowermost level of society: their life expectancy is low, infant mortality and high school dropout rates are high, and many members of the community are drug addicts. Living in paradise is, unfortunately, not paradise at all for them.

Jason, whom I am meeting, moved here years ago from the east coast of the mainland. He built his own house in the rainforest and has been living without money for a long time. As I am waiting for him on a street corner just outside of Hilo, a car stops and the two locals inside eye me grimly. Feeling uneasy, I look away until they drive off. Jason finally comes with his truck and together we travel through the rainforest.

At this point, I begin to wonder if it is a smart idea to make this kind of trip with this guy since I just briefly met him on the internet, but it's too late now. We travel deeper and deeper into the wilderness until we come to an area that has been cleared for Jason's house. His property and lifestyle are phenomenal: he has built a wooden house on stilts four yards high, gets his electricity from solar panels, purifies river water in a self-made cleaning device, showers in an unimaginably beautiful waterfall near his house, and feeds himself from the fruits and vegetables in his garden.

Jason has lived here for two years without any expenses and still has a mobile phone and a pick-up truck. He tells me that he gets his things through bartering and trade; even gas for his truck. In exchange for gas, he lets his dogs hunt for wild pigs in the forest and gives the kill to his friend at the gas station. He does the same with his prepaid mobile phone, which is charged to his friends in exchange for the vegetables he has grown.

We sit over a cup of coffee exchanging our stories. He tells me that he was nervous about our meeting, because he fears that the local government could have him expelled from this property for building a house without permission. All it takes is one nosy journalist searching for a story to trigger a bad chain reaction.

Later, I visit an artist café in Hilo, which is run by a young local. When I was in Oahu I received a few dollars as a gift, so I now use that to buy a coffee—and even give a dollar tip! It occurs to me that the owner didn't greet me and also didn't thank me for the tip. When I move a chair to sit more comfortably, she coldly asks me to use another one. It becomes clear to me that issue here is not the chair but the tension between the locals and white people—in this case, me. When I plug my laptop into the socket at the table, she asks me to leave the café and kindly charge my device at home.

I learn that the Kanaka Maoli people only wish to live again as an independent country. The bronze statue of the last Hawaiian queen in the center of Hilo is a clear symbol of this. Unlike the Inuit in Alaska and the Native Americans in the other states, the Kanaka Maoli do not have any reservations, but they are fighting for that. For many years, the singer Israel Kamakawiwo'ole was the musical mouthpiece of the Hawaiian cause; with his songs, he made the almost forgotten language of *O-lelo Hawa* popular again. Affectionately called the Gentle Giant, Israel died in 1997 of chronic obesity. Ironically, he is best remembered for his versions of the American classics "Somewhere over the Rainbow" and "What a Wonderful World."

For the Hawaiians, the 50th anniversary of statehood in 2009 was not an occasion to celebrate. However, with President Barack Obama hailing from Hawaii, they may now have an important ally for their cause.

The next evening, Lacey Ann, who comes from an old Hawaiian family in Hilo, takes me in. She makes a point of taking in a lot of foreigners and white people in order to introduce them to her local friends: this is her contribution towards *rapprochement.* She has also become more familiar with American culture. I meet her family and her friends, all of whom receive me warmheartedly. Meanwhile, during dinner, her brother-in-law Ja tells me proudly that his fourth great-grandfather was involved in the assassination of explorer James Cook at the end of the 18th century. I take it as a joke, until all of his relatives in the room nod their heads in approval. Some even clap their hands as a sign of pride.

Curiously, I look online and discover that Captain Cook was indeed killed on his third expedition in the late 1770s by a mob of locals on Big Island, the reason being a violation in the agreement between his crew and the locals.

However, legend also has it that Cook and his men spread sexually-transmitted diseases across the island, which killed about half of the original local population. Believe what you will.

Back in Oahu, when Cassandra found out I would be coming to the Big Island, she connected me with her friend Veronica, who lives here. So that afternoon, I meet up with Veronica and she takes me to the primeval forest located to the south of Hilo in the region of Puna. It is known for being one of the most famous hippie areas in the United States. We travel in her SUV on a dirt road through the thick jungle for almost 45 minutes until we reach our destination. We see that a house is in the middle of the forest, approximately 50 by 65 feet, without walls and half covered with furry carpet. The vegetation is so thick that the trees protrude into the house. The residents call this house the Playground: about 30 hippies romp about in the evening, some playing instruments while others do aerial acrobatics on the fabric hanging from the ceiling. One actually hangs head first from this fabric at about 13 feet above the ground and plays the saxophone. Others paint or dance to the music.

During the entire evening, I don't see anyone drinking or doing any drugs, and there are only a few smokers. The only thing one can overdose on here is free vegetarian food. I'm glad that I have come to such an artistic and peaceful place, but then things start to get a little odd. All of us stand in a circle holding hands and dance together to the music. We form the shape of a heart with the human circle, then back to a circle, and then back to a heart again. Then it's time for a partner exercise called Energy Hugs. I stand in front of a guy my own age who has long hair and very much resembles John Lennon. We are encouraged to hug each other and feel the energy of the other person; however, all I feel are the buttons on his corduroy suit pressing into my chest.

Around midnight I leave with Veronica and her friend Natalie. During the drive back, I listen from the backseat of the Jeep as the two women talk about *energy*, which, when translated from hippie jargon to plain English, basically means *sex*. Veronica says, "Devan just got done massaging me in that place. He's given me so much energy."

"Energy is soooooo great. I've been getting so much energy from James. It's been sort of freaking me out though, because he's been getting kind of obsessed with me lately," replies Natalie.

"You'd better be careful," warns Veronica. "Obsession can totally sap your energy."

"True, but there's also Marc, who totally gives me energy on a regular basis."

"What? Are you serious? So tell me, how was it the last time he gave you energy?"

"He gave it to me straight through the night and into morning," Natalie confesses. "It was amazing, even better than what Blake and Dan could come up with."

"It sounds like you should get more energy from Marc. I'm lucky; I've been totally satisfied with the energy I've gotten from Devan and Tim lately."

The only one this evening who doesn't get any *energy* is me. The next day, I hitchhike to continue further. Everywhere, huge clouds of steam are rising up from the landscape; an unbelievable spectacle of nature. The volcanic group of islands is still bubbling violently. In fact, just about 18 miles southeast from here, a new island is forming that already has a name: Loihi. Although Loihi lies about 3,280 feet below sea level, it is expected to be seen in approximately 20,000 years—allegedly, the real estate prices on Loihi are already outrageous.

On the way back I meet Brandon, who is in his mid-twenties. For more than two years now, he has been procuring his food from the primeval forest. This is good because outside of the cities there are no shops where I can ask for food. First, we go for the countless coconuts that have fallen from the palm trees. The coconuts that have 10- to 15-inch long seeds taste the best. We open them with a machete and scratch out the extremely tasty coconut cream. Afterwards, Brandon lists the fruits that grow out here in the wild: papaya, mango, bananas, and so on.

We go through the forest and the pastures and collect various edible flowers. They all look so beautiful, too beautiful to eat; then again, I am very hungry. A long time ago there were more than 50,000 plant species growing on Hawaii, but only 2,000 species still remain today. If I continue at the rate that I am consuming these tasty flowers, there may soon be only 1,999 left. Thanks to Brandon's guidance, the next day I have another fruitful meal (literally) with flowers as my dessert—a healthy diet for a change.

Flower child: Big Island, Hawaii

Sadly, it's my last day in Hawaii. I decide to undertake one of the biggest tourist attractions on the island: Mauna Kea, which stands almost 14,000 feet high. The complete view from the top must really be magnificent—no wonder a tour costs 200 dollars. Although I could have hitchhiked from Hilo to the top of the mountain via the Sattle Road, I decide against it; I have heard various stories about hitchhikers disappearing. Since I still have some money left from the pillow fights, I try to bargain a special price with the taxi driver, Albrecht, who moved to Hawaii from Berlin in 1969. He agrees to take me to the tourist center at the half point of Mauna Kea for a good price.

On the way, Albrecht tells me about his life. In 1969 he packed his bags, moved to Hawaii, and, shortly thereafter, married a Korean woman and had three kids. Fifteen years later, his wife left him and their kids and eloped with another man. When he lost his job as a mechanic, he had to sell his house in Honolulu and move to a shabby colony in the suburbs with the kids, and ever since, he has been working as a taxi driver.

Albrecht is now 73 years old. He gets a small pension from the German government; however, due to the high standard of living here, he must earn another 2,000 dollars every month to make ends meet. Albrecht tells me wistfully that he would love to be in Berlin again. A good German beer at the local bar with a few old friends is just what he desires, but since his three kids all live here and are now married with their own families, his only option is to stay put.

From the tourist center I hitchhike further to the top. The surrounding vegetation changes at every step and at about 11,500 feet I break through the clouds. At the top of Mauna Kea the view is absolutely stunning. I can see all the way past the neighboring island of Maui to far off into the Pacific Ocean. The air is extremely thin and each step is strenuous, but definitely worth it.

The next morning I fly back to San Francisco from Hilo. With a heavy heart I take leave of Hawaii and board the plane. It rains during my stopover in Honolulu, which is nothing unusual—it rains frequently here, but for shorter periods of time. The locals have a special name for this rain, which falls only near the capital city: liquid sunshine.

I still have four nights before my flight to Costa Rica. I log on to the internet to do a Google search for possible groups or institutions in San Francisco that offer a free night's stay: the Club of War Veterans, the Society of Bisexual Women and the Self-Help Group of Excessive Smokers may not be the right ones to approach. I then come across some information for the Hare Krishna temple in Berkeley, and enthusiastically send them an e-mail.

I get a response almost immediately welcoming me to stay with them. Once I get to the temple I am greeted by people wearing the customary Hare Krishna garments.

Their heads are also partly shaven, with pigtails on the sides, and they have golden brushstrokes painted on their foreheads. I meet the leader, who calls himself Gran Torasch. He gives me a bed in a large dormitory and invites me for two meals a day.

While we are kneeling in front of the statue of Krishna, he tells me that the disciples of the group also know very well a life without money since they surrender their possessions to the religious community. For them, possession is opposed to strong belief. He considers my trip without money a very spiritual act, one that will bring me closer to God and remove all impurities. I am not sure whether this is true, but lately, I have been weighing the importance of possessions in my life, especially after my time in Hawaii. So many people have generously given me things these last few months without expecting anything in return. I would like to return the favor one day even if that's only possible after this trip.

In fact, one thing occurs to me: that the media portrays the world as being full of tragedies, violence, war and bad people. But, if all that were true, my trip would never have even been possible. I am extremely thankful and intend to share my positive experiences with others, and let them know that there are many, many great things and people still in the world. Of this, I am absolutely certain.

In the evening we gather in front of the Krishna statue in the chanting room. Everyone bows in front of

Krishna—who, by the way, is half-man and half-woman—and sings over and over: "*Hare, hare Krishna, hare, hare, hare, hare!*" Joining in, I start to relax. After these long three months, a little time off is badly needed. Thanks to the board and lodging of the temple, I can afford to sit around in Berkeley all day without having to worry about food, money, or shelter.

Berkeley itself is just six miles away from San Francisco and is best known for its university, UC Berkeley, and for the protest culture that has been rooted here since the sixties. It is an extremely liberal place, where one can protest everything and anything, which is something I become convinced of while I am on campus one afternoon. A woman in a veil appears with three others dressed up as Guantanamo prisoners wearing orange-colored uniforms, handcuffs, and black cloths over their heads. The woman in the veil suddenly shouts, "Osama is our god!" and "Your fucking president!" Then, she jumps around wildly, throws herself on the ground, plays dead, jumps up again and starts screaming. The police and the students nearby seem unfazed. She tries to provoke them, but no one feels attacked. It's a tough crowd. The woman soon realizes this and retreats, disappointed.

Since I still have two days left before I depart to Costa Rica, I spend this time with Murph and Bryan in Vacaville, which is about an hour's drive from San Francisco. Murph picks me up in his car, and I can luckily count on both of them for free board and lodging. I also get a chance to thank Murph's dad for the flight ticket to

Hawaii. In fact, I even have time to do a favor for Bryan: he teaches geography and history at a nearby high school and asks if I could be a guest speaker for three of his geography classes one day and share my traveling stories. Since I do know my geography and I'm always looking for new experiences (both good and bad), I agree.

Bryan starts his lessons and I wait just outside the door. He asks the 16-year-old students whether they have ever met a German before. The entire class is quiet and shakes their heads. Inevitably, one student calls out that he has seen pictures of Adolf Hitler. While everyone is laughing, I come in and say in German, "Good morning, what's going on in America?" The surprised students laugh at the foreign words. Once we break the ice, the students start bombarding me with questions, all of which I answer as clearly and politely as possible.

After my successful act as guest teacher at Vacaville High School, Bryan takes me that evening to the San Francisco International Airport. As I am waiting for my flight, I do some calculations and realize that I have already covered more than 12,000 miles. Now Latin America awaits me.

10/ On the Run from Dr. Luck
(Costa Rica to Panama)

Oh, how nice: Panama

Although I have two connecting flights on my way to Costa Rica, the trip passes quickly and without problems. It's a funny feeling to fly over the Rocky Mountains one hour, then over the South Coast in the next when it took me weeks to make my way from Ohio to the West Coast. I also find that flying is naturally relaxing; but also, accordingly, boring.

When I land in San José, the capital of Costa Rica, my tension starts to come back. I have no place to stay for the night and the parks are not very inviting for sleeping in at night. Although San José has a population of just 340,000 people (which makes it look like a village if compared to other Latin-American cities like Caracas or Mexico City) there is a very high crime rate. At a nearby newsstand I catch a glimpse of the front page of a tabloid paper showing a close-up photo of a dead body. I look even closer at the disfigured victim in the image: lying in a large pool of blood, the victim had received several shots to his upper body and one to the face.

The press here seems to be much cruder than in Europe, where brutal and violent photos are not printed. I read the caption of the photo and can translate only one word: *violencia,* or violence. I start to get nervous, because I still don't know where I am going to sleep and I want to avoid wandering through San José at night without money. However, despite the capital city, the rest of the country has a good reputation.

Costa Rica is often called the Switzerland of Central America: firstly, because it resembles a tropical version of Switzerland with its mountains and forests; secondly, because things here are economically quite stable and relatively peaceful. In 1983, the then-president, Álvarez, proclaimed permanent and active neutrality, which most likely caused the relative calmness. There is also no official army, either, in this country. For these reasons, I am confident that I will be able to make my way by hitchhiking outside of the capital city.

I have sent over 20 inquiries for overnight stays in Costa Rica and Panama via couchsurfing.com, but have received only one response in Panama City. Therefore, there is nothing else for me to do but leave San José immediately and travel to the capital of Panama, and fortunately, hitchhiking goes better in Costa Rica than in the United States. Still, I am annoyed with myself for not having done a little more pillow fighting while there. A bus ticket from San José to Panama City costs only 30 dollars, which would have been three hours of ludicrous pillow fighting in San Francisco.

I spend the first night in a truck that travels along the coast of Costa Rica. During the following day, cars, a school bus, and a *Colectivo* private minibus take me along. These minibuses are built to hold a maximum of ten people, but usually up to twenty people crowd into them. It is currently the rainy season in southern Costa Rica and there is a downpour nearly every hour. The roads are not fully paved and have large potholes, so the streets are now filled with huge pools of water. I frequently have to take cover and wait for the rain to stop. During these moments, I get to observe the lively street life.

Later on, I come across mountains almost 13,000 feet high that are covered in rainforest to a large extent; I read in a brochure that 27 percent of the land in Costa Rica is protected. As I head along the coast towards the southeastern part of the country, beautiful beaches and palm trees appear for as far as I can see. I make it to the border of Panama just before nightfall, and spend the night at the bus station.

I pass the next twelve hours happily waiting on the station's hard, cold seat. I have been given a free bus ticket to Panama City by the ticket agent; nothing, but nothing can ruin my mood. The 50 plastic seats are all facing a large television screen on which advertisements are running in an endless loop. Most of the commercial spots seem to be bought up by a local cosmetic surgeon, Dr. Paul Alegria—which means *Dr. Luck*. Every 10 minutes his commercials shout out the benefits of his cosmetic surgery to the people in the waiting room. Dr. Luck appears to be a very ambitious cosmetic surgeon; he even offers silicone implants for men so that they can increase the look of their chest muscles and biceps. Just as I am seriously considering this procedure, I fall asleep. I occasionally get woken up by Dr. Luck's voice and by my shivering body. The one air conditioner in the room makes it feel as though I'm already in Antarctica, and even putting on everything I have is of no help.

Before boarding the bus the next morning, I discover from the lady at the ticket counter why she gave me a free ticket. Having grown up in very poor conditions, she often didn't know whether or not she would eat day-to-day. Her relatives, friends and neighbors had all shown her kindness during those hard times and had helped her. Now that she is able to earn her own money, she wants to return the favor and help other people.

On the bus, the air conditioner is running at full blast and it is as cold as the waiting room. Though there is no Dr. Luck here, the stereo's bass system thumps for eight straight hours. Like the television, a limited set of songs play over and over again. The most popular one is a current hit from Panama, which combines salsa, reggaeton, pop, and hip-hop. However, the entire time, I only hear the words "*Humba, Humba, Tätera.*"

Sitting near me is Roger, a 52-year-old American, who migrated to Panama six months ago. He is on the run; not from the police, but from a swine flu vaccination. He is convinced of a conspiracy between the American government and the pharmaceutical industry: the vaccination will only cause other diseases and, as a result, the pharmaceutical companies and government officials will become richer. To avoid falling for this insidious trap, he sold his butterfly collection and relocated to Panama City.

When I express my skepticism, he smiles tolerantly and says, gently, "You must be naive about these matters because you're still young." It ends up being a very educational bus trip. I learn about the many parallels between the U.S. government and the Nazi regime; that Roger's grandfather sighted a UFO in the forties; and that the end of the world is near (which he confirms by taking a Bible from his bag and showing me the psalms where it states this).

Panama City reminds me of Miami with its countless buildings along the water and American fast-food chains on every corner. The Americans occupied Panama at the start of the 20th century and initiated its separation from Colombia. Thereafter, they started to build the rather astonishing Panama Canal, which was inaugurated in 1914. The revenue from taxes (ships pay duty in order not to travel around the whole of South America) had an overall effect on the national income: whereas the average monthly salary in Costa Rica is 600 dollars, in Panama it's almost 1500 dollars, making it easily the richest country in Central America.

The growth of Panama's relationship with the U.S. and their distancing from Colombia led to the abolition of the border checkpoint between the two countries. Panama and Colombia are completely separated from each other by the Darién Gap, an area of primeval forest almost 125 miles wide; it is the last gap of the Panamericana, the road that connects Alaska with Tierra del Fuego. Unfortunately, this lack of a border crossing makes my trip from Panama to Columbia considerably more difficult. I ask the locals whether there is any small border checkpoint for tourists, but all of them shake their heads vigorously. Anyone venturing into the Darién region runs the risk of falling into the hands of Colombian rebels or drug smugglers.

First things first: I decide to stay at Roger's and sort it all out from there. Roger leaves me the house key in his mailbox. Incredibly, after exchanging only a couple of messages on couchsurfing.com, he trusts me to stay there for five days on my own, and lets me help myself to his fridge. His house, secured with metallic grills and fences, has a washing machine, dryer, 500 television channels, and, most importantly, internet. Feeling completely rested, I begin tackling the border issue. I contact the German Embassy and send them an e-mail detailing my problem; I immediately get a reply, and the next day I am sitting in one of their offices.

On the telephone in front of me is written *CAUTION: This phone is not secure. RISK OF INTERCEPTION!* I feel a little like James Bond on a secret mission awaiting news from the ambassador; well, it is true that I am actually waiting for the German ambassador. The ambassador greets me and takes me to his impressive office. He shows great interest in my travel project and begins asking questions: "Why are you doing this? What do you do for a living in Germany? How is the trip so far? Are you having fun?" I stammer while replying because I am nervous—he is, after all, the German ambassador. He tells me that, on the coming Sunday, there will be a garden party held at the *Residencia Alemana* in honor of the parliamentary elections of the Bundestag. Not wanting to miss an opportunity, I offer him my assistance as a butler for the party.

When I arrive at the garden party that Sunday, I see a large yellow board with the Federal Eagle and the inscription: *Federal Republic of Germany*; I am now entering German territory in the middle of Panama. Behind the gate, the stately premises are made up of a swimming pool, a large entrance hall, and a spacious living room and reception room. The Residencia Alemana is furnished in style. During the party I wear a white shirt with stand-up collar, a silver-gray vest, a black bow tie and black trousers. I serve the guests with a silver tray, mainly rosé and white wine. In the background, the future German vice-chancellor celebrates his win in the elections with Chancellor Angela Merkel on several television screens via DW-TV.

Then, the wife of the ambassador takes me aside: my glasses are not filled properly. Wine glasses should be neither half-full nor two-thirds full; they should be exactly 55 percent full. With the wife being French, I have to admit without protest that she is right as far as wine measuring is concerned. But how am I supposed to learn exactly how much is 55 percent of a wine glass? She tells me politely, but firmly, at least ten more times, that the wine glasses are either too full or too empty. I try my best to reach the 55-percent mark exactly and try not to become nervous during my numerous failed attempts. For the time being I manage it, but then I stumble while I am serving the wife of the French ambassador; wine spills out of the glass and the 55 percent quickly become 47 percent. The guests look a little piqued, but a Cologne businessman saves the situation by laughingly telling the guests, "The boy can make it!" The French ambassador's wife smiles; however, the ambassador is a little nervous about what I am up to.

I promised to write only the truth: the ambassador pays me from his own pocket and doesn't waste time with figuring out taxes.

I later meet Mr. Foerster at the party. He is an agent for German opera singers and is currently organizing the first performance of Mozart's *The Magic Flute* in Panama City. For his show he still needs a choir singer (or, more specifically, an extra who can stand on stage in a costume and open and close his mouth). I most certainly know how to stand around blankly while opening and closing my mouth; I accept his offer and find myself that same evening standing on the stage of the city theater among nine other choir boys.

The theater resembles the old German and Austrian ones: balcony seats along the high side walls, gold leaf accents, seats made out of red fabric. The ceiling, painted with angels, clouds and figures, was expertly done— Michelangelo would probably not have been able to do better. The performance goes off without any problems, as the choirboys sing and I just open and close my mouth without any sound. Mr. Foerster stands behind a panel and indicates to me how I should behave; he seems to be under the impression that I am somewhat clumsy. This is not entirely without good reason, because while I am entering the stage I step on my gown and get stuck; the choirboy behind me then runs directly into me. It is bordering on slapstick. I see the appalled face of Mr. Foerster, which only relaxes when finally I leave the stage.

With the pay from my day's work, I book myself a flight. The Colombian airline, *Avianca*, is offering a special, and I have enough money for a ticket to Lima. The flight spares me over 2,100 miles of strenuous land travel through Colombia, Ecuador and northern Peru: a total of two weeks of travel. This eases my mind greatly; after all, I have only six weeks left to reach Antarctica. Still, there is almost 4,300 miles from Lima to Tierra del Fuego, in which I will go through the Andes, the Atacama desert in Chile and the bitterly cold Patagonia in Argentina.

The flight also means, for me, that I no longer have to go through dangerous southern Colombia, an area still quite notorious for its kidnappings by a guerilla group operating out of the rainforest in the South and the East. The killing statistics in Colombia are unsettling: every year more than 20,000 people are killed in this country, the main cause being drug crime. Seventy percent of the cocaine sold worldwide is grown in Colombia. Despite these shocking facts, I don't want to completely miss out on Colombia, and so I decide to make a five-day layover in Cartagena. It should be an adventurous trip.

11/ Katarina's Catamaran (Colombia)

After landing in Cartagena, another passenger drives me into the city. I instantly come across some shady characters. One of them asks me, "What should a *gringo* like you want here?' In order not to become quickly labeled as a European, I take my bag to the park and unpack a black-colored wig and a large mustache. Along with this disguise, I put on pilot's sunglasses and wear a white shirt with my black butler trousers. I test out my new identity and wander in the direction of the old city. Some passersby look at me a little curiously: a six-foot-tall Latino wearing a traveler backpack is probably a rare site around here. Moreover, the mustache and the wig, which are from a costume shop in Cologne, probably give everybody reasons for doubt.

Cartagena is one of the oldest cities of South America and was founded by the Spaniards in 1533. The imposing cathedral, which towers above the city with its large dome, was built a few decades after the arrival of Christopher Columbus. Many other buildings in the old city, the great wall around it, and the fort in the center are also from this period. The residential houses have big wooden balconies and the narrow lanes remind one of Seville or Florence. The residents saunter on the streets and in the parks and enjoy their coffee in the evening sun. Very attractive women smile at me. Salsa blares from many pubs and cafes. Life appears to play itself out on the road.

However, the presence of police and the military here cannot be overlooked or ignored, as large, armored emergency vehicles are parked at the street corners and uniformed cops are present everywhere, including the beach. It is a bizarre picture: tourists sit in their small beach tents, and standing directly near them are soldiers with their machine guns at the ready. In the city center I observe a shoplifter being pursued through the park with a lot of public interest. He is floored by three cops and left lying for twenty minutes in handcuffs and with a bloody face. A man among the bystanders tells me that this is solely for the purpose of demonstrating the strength and determination of the police. Now, this actually takes away my fear of becoming a victim of a robbery, but I still don't want to spend the night outdoors. For this reason, I start looking for possible places to stay and approach some passersby.

One man tells me politely that his relatives are visiting and that he can't oblige me. A young woman refuses because she is still living with her strict Catholic parents. However, she gives me her e-mail address and invites me for a free boat ride. Then I approach a woman sitting in a cyber café. She listens to my story and promptly says, "Of course, we'll make a room free for you. Five days should be fine." I am totally flabbergasted.

Nora lives with the 13 members of her family in a single-story house that has six rooms. Every last one of them gives me a hearty welcome. The first one is Farides, the 25-year-old daughter, who is quickly pushed away by her 28-year-old sister, Dajain. Dajain is holding her 3-year-old daughter in her arms, who very officially shakes hands with me. Farides's daughter, Maya Paula, follows directly after her with a shy *"hola."* Maya Paula's grandmother is next, and sits in her wheelchair while critically looking me over. Thereafter, the great aunt edges through the narrow corridor, smiles at me, and then hugs me as if her long-lost son has come back. After this, the grandfather José Louis, the father, Roberto, and Nora's brother, Eso Maria, greet me. I have to wait some time before Ingrid, Nora's sister, and her two kids conclude the greetings.

There are two to three people staying in each room. As far as furniture is concerned, there are almost only double beds and I don't see any cupboards anywhere. Since the only television in the house is present in the room where I am allowed to sleep, the entire family sits all around me until late into the evening. During the day, the grandmother lies alone on a mattress watching soccer. She is an ardent fan of Real Madrid and watches every game. I try to strike up a conversation with her, but she is not in the mood to talk. Silence is called for when *futbol* is on. For the next five days, we spend six or seven hours in that room together; we don't speak a word while the Spanish and the Colombian league matches are being shown. Even when there is a goal, she remains silent and only raises her hands briefly to express her joy. When the opponents score a goal, she moves her hand from right to left through the room to show her resentment.

Everyone contributes something to the family budget. Nora and her husband are responsible for the food, her sister and her brother for electricity and water, the grandmother and the great aunt for the repair costs. Money is short; Farides even had to discontinue her studies, because she could no longer pay the tuition fees. She now sees her future in the cyber café that the family runs. I am touched that this family, what with their own money problems, agreed to take me in without any reservations or hesitations. For the next five days, they also give me a meal every evening.

During the day I search for food using my tried and tested techniques—my first attempt in Latin America. I visit cafés and shops and ask for small things in order not to lose any more weight on my journey. Since the start of my trip in Berlin, I have lost about 16 pounds. As expected, my success rate in Colombian shops is much lower than in the United States. In the U.S., normally eight out of ten shops offer me something to eat, while here it is only three out of ten who have something to give away (a small bottle of water or a bar of chocolate). Unfortunately, then, offers of complimentary food are a rarity. The main reason for this is probably my inadequate knowledge of the language. My Spanish is simply bad; before starting my trip, I was vain enough to think that I spoke Spanish fluently, but now I realize that I speak only utter nonsense. The people mostly only get bits and pieces: they hear end of the world, about money and food, they hear Germany again and again, and finally don't know at all what to do with any of it. Many of them refer to their boss uncertainly, who won't be in the shop again until tomorrow.

Adding to this is something else: in some shops there are people who are very happy if they earn ten or twenty dollars in a day. Therefore, they are understandably reserved in giving something to a traveler from a rich European country. Still, the gifts I receive are sufficient to pull me through without being hungry; the ones who do understand my Spanish, and already seem to have enough, give a lot so that I can sit again at a restaurant in Colombia.

Due to the heat and humidity, I have to drink a lot and refill my water bottle repeatedly from water taps and fountains. I have chlorine tablets with me from Germany and use them to clean the water. In the part of the city known as Boca Grande I meet Katarina again, the girl who had given me her e-mail address and offered me a ride on a boat. She is 19 and her father is the president of the Sailing Federation of Colombia. In Boca Grande, I feel as if I am once again in Miami. There are modern skyscrapers with mirrored facades, Jeeps and German luxury cars are everywhere, and large yachts lie in the harbor. Katarina is a professional sailor and is aiming to qualify for the next Olympic Games.

After we eat our fill in the sailing clubhouse (at her father's expense), we set out on her catamaran to an island on the outskirts and land in Boca Chica. I'm struck by the unbelievable class difference of the country: poor village dwellers and their children run towards us begging; between the brick houses are provisional wooden and sheet metal structures; the roads resemble mud pits. I guess that the value of Katarina's catamaran exceeds that of the whole village. At the edge of the village there is an imposing fort, which the Spaniards built in the middle of the 16th century. It towers above the palm-lined sand beach.

At every corner one sees group of men and women sitting and playing queen, chess, bingo, dominoes, cards, or Ludo. Playing board games is no game in Colombia: it is serious business. It takes some hours to get ourselves included in the groups in order to play, and it then that I naturally come across a problem: almost all of them are playing for money. Even when the stakes are very low (mostly just a few cents), it is still too much for me. Finally, an exception is made just for me, and I am allowed to use stones that I picked up from the beach. A dominoes player explains to me that playing without money doesn't make any sense, because the use of money triggers the right emotions.

On the beach I start a conversation with a young woman who earns her money with a homemade skin cream that she invites passersby to sample. In this way, she earns just about 300 dollars a month; she and her little daughter live on that. She doesn't have any other options, and tells me that the economic situation is simply too bad. Despite this, she is not envious of the upper class, because she draws happiness and satisfaction from her faith and from her love for her daughter.

Leaving Colombia unexpectedly becomes difficult for me: the welcoming large family, the life on the streets, the beautiful architecture, the nice beaches, and of course, the openness and warmth of the people have all moved and surprised me in only good ways.

12/ My Life as a Peruvian
(Peru to Bolivia)

Romanticism of the Andes meets kitsch of tourism: Peru

Right after arriving in Lima, the capital of Peru, I decide to play my wild card. After all, every game has a joker, right? Mine is called Karina, a 34-year-old Peruvian. We met precisely 10 years ago when I was visiting Peru, and have just recently reconnected on Facebook. She invited me to stay with her for three days in the northern part of town, and it's great to see her again after 10 years: we hug, quickly rattle off details of the last ten years of our lives, and then hop aboard one of the innumerable, overloaded miniature buses at the airport. These buses really are miniature—meant for 20 people at the very most. Instead of sitting, people stand tightly pressed up against each other, easy for the Peruvians (they're hardly ever taller than 5-foot-5). However, for me—at six feet tall—it's horrible. For half an hour, I am stuck with my head uncomfortably bowed, looking out the window.

The drive through the north of Lima offers a rather sad view: the streets are overcrowded, and cars and buses keep honking. Wherever I look, the traffic jams are interspersed with people selling chewing gum, spun sugar, fruit, or even old car parts. People keep squeezing onto the bus trying to peddle their goods there as well. Hardly any houses have plastered walls. We pass endless streets with semi-finished brick houses that have metal rods pointing up from their flat roofs. The few trees I spot are covered in dust. Lima is located in a desert complete with brownish, sandy dust that drowns every bit of green, and I see the same dust on the unfinished houses, cars and buses as well. I breathe it in along with the soot from the many diesel engines in town.

They say Lima is caught under an eternal pall of smog and hardly gets any sun at all. That's just what it's like today: a gray veil covers the sky, making dusty Lima and its 7.5 million inhabitants look even sadder. The difference between Lima and Cartagena is shocking to me. Karina says that Peru still has huge problems with poverty: the average wage is 400 dollars per month; more than one third of the population is poor; and every eighth person even suffers extreme poverty. I look at the faces of the chewing gum vendors on the overcrowded minibus. Some, I see, are quite desperate. They keep begging me to buy at least a single piece of gum for a bargain price. I'm deeply relieved in a very sad way when we arrive at the house of Karina's grandmother and close the door behind us.

Her grandmother, uncle, and son welcome me. With the ever-present lack of money, the term *patchwork family* takes on a completely new meaning here. Karina's uncle, Miguel, who lives on the roof in a shabby, windowless brick shed, isn't her uncle at all. The man just appeared one day at her doorstep ten years ago, completely broke, and has been allowed to live on their roof free of charge out of sympathy ever since. Karina's son is not her son, but her sister's. She usually leaves him with Karina because she is working 14 hours a day.

Then there is Karina's brother, Claudio, who—strictly speaking—is her nephew as well. His parents are living in the U.S., but he had to return to Peru due to drug offenses and is now unemployed and living off his grandmother's money. Karina informs me during the bus ordeal that her grandmother is a strict Catholic, and since Karina is married to Eduardo, an American, she was only able to get permission for my visit by saying that I was Eduardo's brother. This means that for the next three days, I will be playing her husband's brother without knowing the first thing about him. The grandmother is as hospitable as she is smart. Here's an excerpt from our conversation:

"Michael, how is Eduardo at the moment?"

"Oh, quite okay."

"What? I thought he was very sick?"

I hesitate. "Oh, yes, but he's better now. Everything's fine again!"

"Really? Two weeks ago he sounded quite different."

"Well…sure, but last week he got much better."

"Remind me: what was wrong with him?"

Stumbling, I say, "The…many trips abroad…with the military…weakened him. But the doctor saw to that now."

"Yes, poor Eduardo. But didn't he have something wrong with his appendix?"

Karina then steps in and answers for me, claiming I don't know the word for appendix because of my bad Spanish.

So I am spending three days with a very welcoming Peruvian family that keeps engaging me in talk about Eduardo: Eduardo's childhood, his training with the military in Arizona, his first meeting with Karina in the American Embassy; Eduardo and his life at the military base in Rammstein, Germany; Eduardo and his big heart; Eduardo and his bad Spanish (they claim it's even worse than mine); and Eduardo and his American football with lots of beer. The days with the family are hardly stress-free, since I have to be on my guard constantly in order to not fall victim to the grandmother's trick questions. At least I manage to play along without being directly exposed. However, I think everyone involved in the conversations about Eduardo knows perfectly well that I am NOT Eduardo's brother, and I am convinced the grandmother enjoys watching me stumble with wrong claims about him. She confirms this when I later leave by calling after me with a sly grin, *"Muchos besos a Eduardo!"*

In addition to all of the storytelling stress, I find Lima characterized by poverty, dust and thick traffic, but I also have pleasant experiences waiting for me as well. Karina tells me that the upscale restaurants in Peru have a tradition where, on your birthday, they give you free ice cream with a candle to blow out while singing "Happy Birthday" to you. This all starts when Karina jokingly points out, in a restaurant where we are not even eating, that it is my birthday. We sit down and, a moment later, five waiters appear before me singing *"Feliz Cumpleanos, Felizidad"* or something like that. They put free ice cream with a candle on the table and a paper crown on my head. We try out this free phenomenon two more times in the quarter of Mira Flores: "Yes, Micha has his birthday today!" Thus, I spend the 13th of October mostly eating free ice cream.

Muy delicioso: birthday feast in Peru

With my three birthday paper crowns, I take bus to the town of Cusco, located more than 600 miles away in the Andes. At less than 30 dollars, the ticket is very cheap and paid for by good old Eduardo all the way from his military base in southern Germany. Karina had told him about my journey with no money, and the resulting problems: my white lies to her grandmother. Since I had been forced to intensely study his life, he decided to pay for my bus ticket as something of a reward. Now I am traveling first class on a Peruvian long-distance bus: I can fold back my seat and turn it almost into a bed; blankets are distributed and the air conditioning is running at full power, like everywhere in Latin America; and I have a TV in front of me with an American movie playing on it. Peruvians seem to particularly enjoy horror and splatter movies: *Friday the 13th*, Stephen King movies, and *Texas Chainsaw Massacre* alternate in the program. The television's volume rivals even that of the air conditioning, making it impossible for me to sleep. At midnight, the Japanese horror movie *The Ring* starts playing; now it's officially impossible to sleep, since this movie is truly one of the scariest horror films that I have ever seen.

The next afternoon I reach the Andes without much rest, but now I'm at least somewhat of an expert in horror films. The city of Cusco lies at an altitude of almost 11,000 feet and is the starting point for trekking tours to the world famous Inca city of Machu Picchu. Cusco is a very beautiful mountain city with two huge missionary churches directly at the marketplace, which everyone in

Peru calls *Plaza de Armas* (Place of Weapons). Narrow streets run through the centuries-old walls of downtown, which was built by the Spaniards after their conquest of Peru.

This is where I meet Stefan, a 34-year-old German whom I had contacted by e-mail before my trip. At the beginning of the year, Stefan had moved from Germany to Cusco; he is now trying to set up an agency called Geomundo, which organizes trekking tours for tourists. He aims to do this in an ecological way and with fair salaries to the local workers. Stefan tells me that it was a difficult decision to give up a well-paying job as a management consultant in order to go and start a business abroad. Here, he is struggling with a different mentality: punctuality, reliability and discipline are not the deciding values for his colleagues. I'm able to spend two nights in his new apartment that has just been renovated and furnished.

Stefan hooks me up with a local trekking agency that is ready to take me free of cost to Machu Picchu...if I carry the baggage for them. A visit to Machu Picchu is naturally in order because the Inca city represents a massive cultural highlight of South America.

Machu Picchu lies 50 miles away from Cusco, in the middle of a rainforest in the mountains. The city was built by the Incas in the middle of the 15th century and was abandoned about 100 years later when the Spaniards conquered the region. Still, it was not the Spaniards who drove the Incas out of the city; even today, it is not clear what happened. One theory is that Machu Picchu was built to control the economy of this region, while another theory considers Machu Picchu as a former prison city of the Incas. Other researchers consider Machu Picchu as the home of the former Inca king. Thus, the origin of the so-called lost city of the Incas still remains a mystery to us.

On the first day, there is a lot of amazement and laughter among the 16 members of the trekking group (who come from Germany, Canada, USA, Argentina, Ireland and France). Even the three local porters are amazed that a *gringo* wants to carry the baggage. How can it be that a German carries food, utensils and tents up the mountain? I explain that I am traveling to the end of the world without any money and that this is the only way I'll be able to see Machu Picchu. The porters laugh and are happy about the unusual support; the tourists laugh at my rather foolish outfit. Before my departure, Stefan had lent me a traditional poncho and a woolen cap with earmuffs and pompoms, but it looks like the only Peruvians wearing this attire are the ones you would find in European pedestrian zones.

I am lucky and get a grace period on the first day of the trekking tour. The porters halve the normal carry load for me from 80 pounds to 40 pounds. However, this weight is not carried as it would (or should) be in a normal backpack, but is instead made up of plastic bags tied together with ropes that are then carried as a makeshift backpack. While the porters run in front at full speed, on the first day I am allowed to walk with the rest of the group at the normal European pace. We cover almost 12 miles and climb from 8,500 feet to the height of 11,800 feet.

Searching for the pedestrian zone:
on the way to Machu Picchu

At around five in the evening, I reach the first *bivouac* shelter with the group and help the porters set up the tents for the tourists and prepare the dinner. The porters have two gas cookers in a small shelter, and for the next two hours, my task is to peel the peas. The evening then becomes a nightmare: while the group can at least sleep protected from the extremely cold temperature in tents, I spend the night with the three other porters in the shelter and only a blue plastic sheet to separate my sleeping bag from the extremely cold, extremely hard ground. Lying near me is Gomerciendo, the cook for the group. I ask him how he endures this and Gomerciendo explains that he only rarely sleeps in beds. While he is snoring away, I remain awake during most of the night; it's noisy, cold, the ground is hard, and the high altitude of 11,000 feet makes me toss and turn all night.

At four in the morning, Gomerciendo's alarm clock rings. We have exactly one hour to prepare breakfast for the group. I sit impassively, shivering in the corner. At six o'clock, the group starts for the second leg of the trip; they have six hours to reach the afternoon stop at the 15,000-feet-high Abra Salkantay pass. The porters have to make it in three hours' time; hence, we have to walk twice as fast, basically running. The reason for this lack of time is that we took 90 minutes to dismantle the tents, wash the utensils, and load up the horses that morning, and the porters must arrive at the next stop 90 minutes before the group does so that we have time to prepare and have lunch ready by the time everyone else arrives.

It quickly becomes clear to me that the decision to go along with the group as a porters and worker was, and is, insane. I can hardly keep up the speed, although I am carrying only half the weight that Gomerciendo, Yuri and Nico have on their backs. After nearly half an hour, I manage to remain standing but pant and bend forward frequently in order to breathe in gulps of air. Yuri asks me to pull myself up and to keep up pace because we are under enormous time pressure; after all, the tourists would like to have their lunch on time. I continue to follow the three porters and the three horses, but physically I am just not able to make it. I am dizzy and my legs feel like rubber.

A short while later I am far behind them. Yuri is up ahead of me as the path goes up the mountain in a serpentine trail. He calls out again and again: "*Amigo, vienes. No tenemos tiempo! Rápido*!" Translated, that is: "Come, my friend, we have no time to lose! Hurry!" But it doesn't help me; the air is too thin and I am not trained. I lie down on the path and breathe in and out deeply. Shortly thereafter, Yuri, Gomerciendo and Nico come down with the horses and look at me hopelessly. Gomerciendo laughs, because he has never seen such an incapable porter in his entire life, but Yuri is annoyed and asks me to stand up. He anxiously explains to me that we need to be at the next camp before the tourists in order to prepare the lunch; if the food is not ready, there will be complaints to the agency and it might cost them their jobs. I realize that I have behaved very carelessly as a porter.

Two evenings ago I had boasted to the boss of the agency (who, by the way, is called Fidel Castro) that I was a thousand-meter runner and that the 50 miles would not be a problem. Now I was a burden on the tour. Due to their care of duty, the porters cannot leave me behind, but also cannot continue to wait for me. I promise them that I will keep up with the pace if we could just buckle up my weight on one of the horses. The three porters consult among themselves and reach the decision that about 20 pounds from my baggage could fit on the horses; any more than this would be unbearable for them, too. So now I carry only twenty pounds up the mountain pass, but the altitude makes it feels like 80 pounds.

Even after this lightened load, I am not able to match the speed of the porters and quickly fall behind. I drag myself through the breathtaking landscape with its snow-covered mountain peaks and glaciers that go up to a height of 20,000 feet, but all these things make no difference to me because I am totally knocked out and overwhelmed. I come across a wooden hut selling chocolate bars and beverages to the trekking enthusiasts. I hear a German couple trying to decide between a Twix and Snickers, and between a large and a small Coke. I am completely envious and can only drag myself frustratingly past them. Oh, the things I would do now for just a two-liter bottle of Coke and a chocolate bar!

It becomes really cold after 13,000 feet, although we are sweating from the strenuous climb. I can no longer see Yuri and the others. Every step seems like a kick in the teeth; the pain penetrates my entire body. After breaking for the second stretch of the day, Yuri tells me that he earns 50 dollars for a five-day trip. I am speechless that the tourists have to pay so little for such an effort on his behalf.

Shortly before the pass at 15,000 feet, I am able to overtake the tourist group. Yuri, Gomerciendo and Nico have passed them long ago with the horses. The leader of the group is taking a special break so that the porters have enough time for cooking (since they have lost so much time because of me). The group cheers when they see me passing them. They know that my experiment has been a total flop but they all take it lightly; unfortunately, Gomerciendo doesn't. When I finally reach the mid-day camp, the food is almost ready and lain out on the tables. Gomerciendo, who is totally pissed off, gives me a lecture about how they can no longer manage having the food ready on time and that something like this could lead to problems with the agency. During the lunch, Yuri takes me aside and tells me that it simply can't go on like this. Further reprieves are made for me: I can continue to work as a porter, but I can walk with the tourist group. This means that the speed is only half as fast and that I don't have to help so much in the kitchen, and in setting up and dismantling the tents—a huge respite for me.

The very next day, everyone's displeasure over the conspicuous gringo porter changes to sympathy. My service from the second day has become something of a legend: I hear the porters as they again and again laughingly tell the story of how I lay panting on my back on the narrow trail.

In this manner we continue on and, on the third and the fourth day, pass a temperate rainforest. There is even a delightful break to relax, and the group takes a bath in one of the hot springs from the Andes. The hot spring near Santa Theresa is commercially used for tourism: one has to pay a five-dollar entry fee, whereas the locals pay only thirty cents. Dietmar, a police commissioner from Heilbronn who is trekking with us, invites me along and pays the entry fee for me. Unfortunately, I catch a cold at the hot springs and on the fifth day, set out at four in morning relatively ill. We have to climb 1,600 steps and about 1,500 feet to reach Machu Picchu. It is, again, a hard struggle to the top.

The previous evening, Yuri had distributed the entry tickets. I assumed that as a porter I wouldn't need one, so I didn't worry about it. Now I stand in front of the entry gate, still dressed in the foolish poncho and the cap and loaded with cargo, explaining that I am the porter and have done the impossible in the last five days. The lady smiles in a friendly way and lets me in without a ticket. Tourists stand in front of and behind me in the long queue, laughing and cheering at the gringo porter entering the Inca city without ticket. But at the second checkpoint, a man pulls me out of the line. He doesn't say a word and radios someone: "*Hay un hombre sin ticket!*" ("There is a man without an entry ticket!") I am brought, or rather, led away to an office. The man throws my baggage on the floor and refuses to answer me.

In the office I talk to the boss who handles visitor relations. I explain to her that I have worked as a porter for five days and hence have the right to enter. She counters that I am obviously a tourist and hence have to pay 43 dollars. I explain that my work as a porter was part of my journey to the end of the world. She tells me that she finds this all great, but that I still have to pay 43 dollars. Even when I offer to collect the garbage in Machu Picchu, she remains unmoved.

Yuri and the tourist group are nowhere to be seen. This is the darkest moment of my trip. I sit in front of the gates of the Inca city totally frustrated: 50 miles with 40 pounds on my back climbing a height that, in comparison, makes the Grossglockner and Mont Blanc seem tiny, and now this! I know that from now on, this journey is going to be really difficult. I still have to cover 3,700 miles and have only three weeks in which to do it. I will be lacking the drive of the initial months, the excitement that I felt in San Francisco and in Hawaii. Even after the muscle cramps, cold, and emotional setback of Machu Picchu disappear, the last 3,700 miles will be anything but easy.

Later, a bus takes me back to Cusco. Stefan has agreed to let me spend one more night with him, and the next morning I will travel from Puno to Lake Titicaca on a train called the *Andean Explorer*.

I am sitting in Stefan's apartment and trying to plan my journey further, when suddenly his stove and chimney catch fire. The chimney is probably not completely made of fireproof material, as within half a minute the apartment is engulfed in flames. We run off to quickly get water from the shower, but the water supply has just been turned off in the entire city (as so often happens in Peru). I run frantically to the neighbor and get a fire extinguisher. We try to spray it, but it doesn't do anything. I then run into the street and explain to a cop in Spanish that a fire has broken out in the apartment, but since I am in a panic, my Spanish is much worse than usual. I repeat again and again: "*Fuego! Fuego!*"

Unfortunately, in this context it only means a light for a cigarette. *Incendio* is the word for an actual fire. The cop only patiently repeats that he doesn't have a light and that he gave up smoking a year ago. In my distress I grab him by his uniform and pull him towards the apartment. Over the rooftops one can hear Stefan shouting, "*Incendio! Incendio!*" The cop now understands what the problem is and calls the fire brigade on his mobile phone. Meanwhile, the fire has spread almost to the entire apartment. I suddenly remember my bag with all my belongings: passport, video cameras, recorded tapes. *Dios mio*. I hold my breath and run through the fire, and luckily find my bag undamaged.

Panting, I come out of the apartment carrying everything out safely. Outside, I stand to the side and watch as the cop rips open all the windows, causing the fire to spread further. Stefan is standing and gasping at the doorway; he has probably inhaled too much carbon monoxide. He is spitting and coughing over and over again. Suddenly, one of the neighbors beckons me. She has a large bathing basin in front of her. Running towards her, I grab the heavy basin, carry it up one flight, and pour the water on the fire. The fire truck arrives and does the rest.

Stefan now has a fire extinguisher in his hand, which works, and extinguishes the last of the flames. I come to learn how relatively lucky we were in our misfortune. The fire broke out at eleven o'clock in the evening; what would have happened if it had been one o'clock in the morning? I help Stefan to sweep up the mess. The apartment is now unlivable: the ceiling is half burnt, the floor is covered with soot and burnt pieces of wood, and the kitchen wall with the sink and cupboards is completely burnt. At three in the morning we bid farewell to each other, both of us still visibly in shock. I spend the last hours of the night at the train station in Cusco waiting for the *Andean Explorer*.

Totally blurry-eyed, I try to make my way the next morning to the platform. The *Andean Explorer* is a luxury train and the eight-hour journey costs 220 dollars. This is ten times as much as the cost of the bus journey for the exact same distance. Every passenger at the station is checked for a ticket. I am checked immediately and sent away in an unfriendly manner, so I drag myself to the bus station, and notice for the first time that a part of my backpack is burnt. What a harrowing night! I decide that I will make use of this stroke of fate at the bus station to get at least a free ticket to Puno. I tell about my five-day trekking, about how I was not able to enter Machu Picchu, and about the fire in Stefan's apartment. Both of the bus employees watch and listen to me blankly, then exchange glances and start smiling. They give me a free ticket without asking any further questions.

The bus travels at an altitude of between 11,000 and 13,000 feet. I see a chain of snow-covered mountains, pastures with llamas, and then finally Lake Titicaca, which is the world's highest crossable lake at a height of about 12,500 feet. But I am not able to enjoy much of the attractions. For one thing, I am totally wrecked physically. For another, I don't know how I am going to get any further on my journey. In order to get information about some opportunities, I ask a tourist couple on the bus if they could briefly lend me their *Lonely Planet* travel guide. The woman gives me the book.

"Of course," she says with a smile. "By the way, we can also talk in German. Tell me…don't we know each other from Cologne? Don't you have a friend by the name of Kristina?"

"Yeah, that's right. We met years ago over a beer, right?"

"Exactly!"

It is said that after every low there comes a high. This is exactly what happens now. I tell my story to Hedwig and her husband Cicki, and we quickly make a deal: they will take care of the costs of my food and my stay in Puno, and buy me a bus ticket to La Paz, Bolivia, if I will chauffeur them around for one day through the area. I am saved!

Sinking ground underfoot: Uru's village on Lake Titicaca

The chauffeuring turns out to be driving a pedal boat. While Hedwig and Cicki are smooching in the back of the boat, I pedal over the huge lake. It is hard work, but is fun. I row both of them to one of the famous Uru islands. The Uru are a tribe that lives on self-made reed islands—their houses and boats are made out of reeds, and at times, reeds are also a part of their diet. We visit one of the islands and

I get an opportunity to talk to the president of the Urus. While nibbling on a reed, he answers my questions.

The Urus moved out to sea even before the time of the Incas, because they could safeguard themselves quickly and effectively against their enemies with their maneuverable reed islands. Nowadays there are a total of 42 reed islands with over 2,000 inhabitants. As one walks onto an island, they can feel themselves sinking into the soft reeds by up to ten centimeters, similar to stepping on a cushion. Every year new reed layers are laid on the floor, because the reeds gradually decay into the water.

The president also tells me that reed is used not just as food, but also as medicine for various diseases. Despite their passion for reed, they are not reluctant to accept modern technology: solar panels, engines, television and a radio transmitter are a part of the daily routine in the village. He tells me that part of the Uru system now also involves living off tourism, but on the more remote islands, one still lives off the barter system. The inhabitants on these islands make reed products and in exchange can get everything that they need for living.

"Where are the people happier?"

The president thinks about this question, and then says that tourism and money naturally bring some disadvantages because of the changes to the culture. But he finds it more important that the Urus, who makes a living from tourism, now have enough money for education and medicine.

Hedwig and Cicki invite me to dine with them several times and also give me 20 dollars. With this, I can afford two nights in a hostel and still buy a bus ticket to Bolivia.

13/ A Kingdom for a Guinea Pig (Bolivia)

The next morning I am sitting with two liters of Coke and two liters of water on the bus to La Paz, Bolivia. At a height of 11,800 feet it is the highest capital city in the world. When we reach the border, my stomach starts growling: I haven't eaten anything since the previous evening. Unfortunately, I don't meet any other generous couples from Cologne, only a drunk Brit who invites me to go boozing. I decline with thanks.

By the time I get to the bus station in La Paz, I have gone 24 hours without food. I immediately begin my search for nourishment, asking a total of 30 kiosks, shops and restaurants in and around the bus station for donations, but am met with no success. A shopkeeper advises me to go directly to the German embassy, since he considers my endeavor in Bolivia pointless.

Statistics prove him right: Bolivia is the poorest country in South America. The average citizen here earns less than 350 dollars a month. However, Bolivia is rich in natural resources: 50 to 70 percent of the world's lithium is found here, and the gas deposits are among the largest on this American continent. But most of the residents of the plateau, where La Paz is located, see very little of this wealth, which also explains the victory in the election of the socialist-backed President Morales. His aim is to achieve a better distribution of money between the rich East and the poor West.

The people appear to me to be withdrawn and cool, quite different from what I saw in Colombia. I become very nervous because my hunger is growing; a pain spreads in my stomach. Luckily, the Coke and a pack of coca leaves, which I chew regularly, suppress the feeling of hunger a little, but the panic remains: should I abandon my attempts here? For emergencies, I have brought my credit card. The trip should not end with me starving in Bolivia, but if I use the credit card even once, then my journey and story would come to a close. The question here, naturally, is not one of survival, but of the goal to bring this project to its desired conclusion.

Meanwhile, it has become dark and it is no longer advisable to wander through the city. Driven by fear, I decide to go back to Peru. Since I am physically exhausted and totally starved, but don't want to end my project here by using my credit card, I see this as the last way out. I go to different ticket counters and relate to them that I am traveling to the end of the world without money and that I am simply at the wrong place in Bolivia to continue such a project.

Both of the first two clerks whom I address immediately agree with me, but send me away without a ticket. The ticket lady at the third bus company also shrugs me off at first, so I go a step further and tell her that I haven't eaten anything for almost 30 hours. When she shakes her head the second time, a man, who is sitting at a computer behind her, intervenes. He seems to be the boss and says something in Spanish that must mean: "Come, let's take him along. He really has nothing!" This assurance is my biggest success in Bolivia.

Since the bus departs very early the next morning, I sleep on a bench in the bus station of La Paz—or rather, doze away in a half-sleep. I feel worn out, I am in a bad mood, and I am no longer hungry. The reason is probably a secretion of adrenaline or endorphins, or my stomach has simply switched over to emergency / survival mode.

The bus is overfull because currently there is a strike in La Paz, and only a few coaches are running. I stand in the aisle. The seated passengers, who boarded the bus in other cities, are having their lunch. I look around to see if someone has something left over—not a chance. However, a man has reclined his seat and is sleeping, and the bus steward has simply placed his lunch on his thighs without waking him up. This is my chance! I gently wake the man up and ask him if I could possibly get his lunch. He looks at me totally dazed; my Spanish only explains the situation in bits and pieces and he is still quite sleepy, but after a second explanation he agrees and gives me the tray.

I have never been without food for almost 40 hours in my entire life; never before have I been so happy about a meal. Although I no longer feel my hunger pangs, I devour the rice, mashed potatoes, piece of meat, and the small gelatin dessert. I am delighted that I trusted myself and asked this man, because the five-hour bus journey becomes a nine-hour one. Due to the strike, the bus driver has to turn off the main roads and drive on dirt roads. Suitcases and bags fall from the overhead compartments, and finally, all of us have to disembark because the bus either cannot or is not permitted to drive on that stretch of road. We wait for another bus for at least two and a half hours in the middle of the plateau. I look towards the horizon and see quite a long traffic jam on the other side of the road towards La Paz. The strike has simply frozen everything.

Arriving finally in Puno, I am still starving. With not a single minute to waste, I run towards the city center where the shops and restaurants are. To my delight, a generous restaurant manager offers me a free meal. Since I'm in Peru, I decide to order the Peruvian delicacy dish: guinea pig. On a plastic tray, my order is served to me with the head and feet still intact, along with a side salad. I sit in front of the restaurant and devour the whole guinea pig—satisfying, although the texture is slightly tough.

Afterwards, I head to Puno's fruit market, located in the harbor. Some of the women in the market still remember me from my last visit a few days ago. I tell them about the dead end in Bolivia and about going 40 hours without food. After hearing my story, every single lady at the stalls starts offering me fruit. Overwhelmed and full of gratitude, I collect all the fruit into a cardboard box. The story quickly spreads around the market and soon, even without a word, I am handed an assortment of bananas, tomatoes, apples, potatoes, onions and pears. After about an hour or so I have canvassed all the stalls in the market and filled the large box.

The fruit and vegetables would probably sustain me for a week if I had a refrigerator, but clearly, I do not. I decide to go to the bus station and try selling the extra produce. In no time I sell everything and earn 17 dollars. With this money, I can now buy a bus ticket to Arica, the northernmost city of Chile. After the Inca trail, the disaster of Machu Picchu, the apartment fire in Cusco, and going 40 hours without food, things can only, *only* get better from here.

14/ The Madman
(Chile)

A foretaste of the end of the world:
The Atacama Desert in Chile

At the bus station of the desert city of Arica, the aunt of a Chilean friend picks me up. She has an empty apartment on the second floor of her house, which I am allowed to use. Every morning I get a sumptuous breakfast; every evening I am fed steaks and other delicacies so that the weight loss of the last two weeks is compensated. Both nights I sleep for twelve hours, something I haven't done in months. My laundry is washed and for the onward journey the aunt packs a plastic bag full of groceries and drinks. It is 48 hours of complete well-being. Unfortunately, I can't stay any longer, since I now have only twelve days to reach Ushuaia, in Tierra del Fuego. La Paz and the victory lap through Puno have consumed an unbelievable amount of time.

I stand on the corner of a street at the town exit with a large cardboard sign, on which I have written *SUR* (*"south"*). Huge sand dunes are present all around me. Hitchhiking goes off well from this point. I never wait any longer than thirty minutes for a lift. Sergio, a truck driver, takes me along through the Atacama Desert. It is the driest desert in the world. Only one-fifth of the total rain quantity in (the extremely dry) Death Valley in the U.S. falls here. The reason for this is that the eastern winds from the continent bring dry air along with them. The Pacific Ocean lies to the west but, because of the extremely cold Humboldt currents, the winds from this direction are mostly rainless. The temperature fluctuations in this desert are also extreme: day temperatures of around 86 degrees

Fahrenheit and night temperatures of around 5 degrees are not rare. I am happy to be able to cross the entire desert with Sergio and not have to sleep in a tent at night.

On the road, Sergio tells me stories about his life. He has two families: one in the north in Arica and one in the capital city, Santiago de Chile, which lies about 1,200 miles to the south. He laughingly says that, according to him, it is completely acceptable for a truck driver to have a family on both ends of his route. For the next 600 miles random cultural topics pop up in our conversation: the big blonde women in Germany, women in Brazil, cigarette prices in Germany, and, naturally, German beer companies versus the ones here in Chile. During the ten-hour drive, we pass huge sand dunes and the desert seems to be endless. After Sergio drops me off, I am taken along to Santiago de Chile by other trucks, vans and cars.

In 30 hours, I have covered over 1,200 miles.

It is spring and the temperature in Santiago is moderate. I head towards the city center where the streets are filled with people. I have very little time for sightseeing, as I have an appointment with Reinhard. He is one of the managers of *Antarctic Dream*, the shipping company and travel agency that has agreed to take me to Antarctica at no charge. The *Antarctic Dream* offers luxury cruises in which many of its passengers are wealthy millionaires coming from all over the world. He explains to me that, during the tour, for the ten days my role is to assist the expedition leader. "And I expect nothing but your best performance," he adds, and I know he means it.

On that same day, I travel on a minibus from Santiago to Buenos Aires, Argentina, over 600 miles away. Earlier, my friend's aunt had me given a care package to take along with me for my journey. The package included an envelope with 25,000 pesos in it—almost 50 dollars. With gratitude, I am able to use 30 dollars of this money to buy the ticket for the minibus. I actually have enough money for the long-distance bus, but I want to save some, thinking this very economical and smart. Later, however, it turns out that this is actually a bad decision. The driver of the minibus is very unfriendly and reckless, and I can hardly enjoy the view as we drive over passes that are 13,000 feet high. Speedy Gonzales here is keeping us on edge: speed limits don't seem to exist and the extreme left curves keep me hanging on to my seat for dear life. I sit directly behind him and cannot keep my eyes off the speedometer.

Finally, I can't take it any longer. In a calm tone I simply point out that he is traveling 30 miles above the speed limit: "*Senor, hay 70 y no 120 kilometros, por favor.*" He immediately yells something back at me, and even turns around and actually *lets go of the steering wheel* to wave his arms in the air for emphasis. After he turns around, there is total silence from everyone. The old man to the right of me looks at him, equally as shocked as I am, but we don't dare say a word.

To take revenge on my protest, the driver inserts a cassette into his tape player, adjusts it to full volume, and systematically tortures us with the strains of Elton John, Meat Loaf and Chris de Burgh. Just when we are nearing another bus, a car cuts across in front of us from the other lane. The people in the car wave at us wildly; the driver of the vehicle starts flashing his headlights. Our driver won't allow this, so he steps on the gas pedal. We pass the car by an absolute whisker. In the background I can still hear the car honking madly.

I blow a fuse and start shouting at this driver. He shouts back, *"Chile, no Alemania! Chile aqui, no Alemania!"* He clarifies for me that here in Chile, the Chilean (not my German) rules apply. It makes no difference to me; I spit out the worst possible insults that my Spanish vocabulary allows in such situations: *"Hombre sin cara!"* ("You're a man without a brain!") The driver turns around and shakes his fist at me while the old man sitting in the front passenger seat tries to calm him down and pulls him forward again. After that, it is silent again in the minibus. I get a hold of myself and think of what I should do. Disembarking in the middle of the Andes is a poor option, because I don't know whether any other car will take me along from here. Yet traveling another 500 miles to Buenos Aires with this guy is also not an option, as the risk of us either getting into an accident, me punching the driver, or both, are very high.

Some time later we stop for a toilet break at a rest stop. I jump off with my luggage and tell the driver of another minibus parked there that I have just traveled with a madman, and ask for him to take me along. The first driver notices what I am doing and starts screaming and threatening to hit me. The driver of the other minibus quickly comes between us and holds him back. The crazy driver yells that I should go back to Germany. I won't accept that and throw it back at him by saying once again that he is a man without a brain.

In the meantime, numerous other passengers gather around us and start laughing. In my hurry, I mix up the nouns and call him "man without a face" instead of "man without a brain." I hear a boy saying ironically that even he wouldn't like to travel to Argentina with a man without a face. Others agree with him and chuckle. In any case, the seriousness of the situation becomes clear to the second driver. He disappears with the driver *without a face,* and shortly afterwards, comes back offering me a seat on his minibus. I can see him still putting away the money he got from the other driver. I am relieved that my commotion has resulted in something. In minibus number two, we travel at normal speed through the Andes to Argentina— the last country of the trip.

15/ Ümit Saves the Day
(Buenos Aires to Tierra del Fuego)

Exactly 0.5 people per square meter: Patagonia

Buenos Aires absolutely takes my breath away. I have always wanted to come here and all the good things I have read and heard about the city are confirmed at first glance. The magnificent house facades in the elaborate architecture of the 19th and 20th centuries—which can easily compete with Paris, Madrid or Rome—shape the overall image of the city; Paris, in particular, appears to have been a big influence on its appearance. The cemetery of the city district of Recoleta, with its tombs, mausoleums and roads, reminds me of the famous Père Lachaise cemetery in Paris. The Argentinean legend and former First Lady Evita Perón is buried here.

Both the Plaza de Mayo, with obelisks as landmarks in the middle, and the early 20th century colorful structures of Avenida 25 de Mayo, resemble the boulevards of downtown Paris. Buenos Aires appears very European to me. However, there is also a whiff of New York because with its population of over ten million people, the city seems to me much bigger and more imposing than any of the European metropolitan cities.

During my five-day stay I don't see any un-plastered or unfinished houses. Even the poverty, which is certainly present here, is not outwardly visible. In the entire time I am there, I see only one beggar. In contrast, the Porteños, as the locals are called, stroll along the Avenidas and walk through parks and sit in the many cafes of the city. Street hawkers, who shape the streetscape in Peru and Bolivia, are nowhere to be seen. Buenos Aires seems to have money; in fact, a lot of it. I am only about 600 miles away from La Paz as the crow flies, and once again, appear to be in quite a different world.

That evening, my impression of the everyday culture being influenced by Italian and Spanish immigrants is confirmed. For the first time in many weeks, I become a couch surfer again. Noelia and her friend Roberto let me sleep at their place for three days. Both of them are 31, work at an advertising agency, dress very smartly, and live in a well-designed apartment. They tell me that most of the ancestors of Argentineans come from Italy and Spain. The Italian influence can also be seen clearly in the language. Like most of Latin America, they speak Spanish here, but the pronunciation has an Italian touch. Their daily rhythm is even influenced by the Italians and the Spaniards.

Noelia and Roberto are at home quite often. They offer me dinner, which is always at eleven in the evening, and on weeknights they plunge into the nightlife of Buenos Aires. I am thankful for their hospitality and return their favor by cleaning their toilets, which I had also done at the aunt's place in Chile. However, I am not in any mood to go out. I am totally exhausted by the trip and had not even been able to enjoy Peru, Bolivia and Chile properly. I would prefer to go to bed at ten, but they both insist that we go out together so that I can get to know the city; and so we go to bed on Tuesday at two in the morning, on Wednesday at three, and on Thursday at around midnight. I feel guilty the entire three days, because I want to offer them something (or someone) more than just a tired tourist traveling with a backpack and no money; but my energy is all used up.

This continues at my next couch station as well. Micaela, Raphaela and Antonella (by the way, all typical Italian names) are all in their early 30's and live in the happening scenic district of Palermo. They offer me the sofa in their living room. I anticipate something bad, and not without good reason; it is the weekend and they want to throw a party at home. At midnight the whole living room shakes, because 40 of their friends have gathered for alcohol and music. Almost all of them are drunk and are vociferously singing along with the songs of the karaoke machine. I can hardly keep myself awake and keep drinking Coke and yerba maté tea in huge quantities so that I don't go to sleep on the floor in the middle of the action. None of it helps, and by two in the morning I feel physically finished.

I tell Micaela that I am going to just lie down on her bed and sleep. In disbelief, she roars with laughter. The next few hours I spend only dozing in the neighboring room; the bass is so loud that my whole body is vibrating. The dozing comes to a premature end after a group of drunken people cruises into the bedroom. I am probably a curiosity for them, and am besieged with offers for drinks while I try to straighten myself up. It finally comes to an end at six in the morning, and I can finally sleep in the living room. The next evening is a Saturday: party day, of course!

This Saturday is, in fact, quite a special party day because it is Halloween. Micaela and Raphaela make themselves up as monsters for the night. After an eleven o'clock dinner, we go to a party at a friend's house. None of my arguments as to why it would be better if I stay at home are accepted as reasonable. Micaela and Raphaela definitely want to celebrate Halloween with their couch surfing guest—no excuses! With a long beard and a pale white face, I stay at the Halloween party of 150 people until eight in the morning. Actually, to be completely honest, I pass out on the couch at four before being taken back home by Raphaela and Micaela at eight in the morning. Still, they cordially bid farewell to me the next day—and crack a few small jokes at my expense.

Along with the five nights in Buenos Aires there are also the five days, which I spend collecting food and finding onward journey options towards Tierra del Fuego. For the third time on this trip I feel the urge to use my credit card: *Oh come on, just this once! It's not a big deal. You deserve a break!* I am sitting in the city district of San Telmo on a bench, and when I take out my passport and my insurance papers from my chest pocket, my credit card falls out and into my hand. Maybe it's a sign! It would make everything so easy. Presto! One swipe through the machine and I am off. I had the same feeling in La Paz, where I desperately needed the card. But there is no shop near the bus station that accepts credit cards. This fact probably prevents me from giving into the temptation. I really don't know what would have happened if someone had cried: "Fresh steaks and we accept credit cards!"

I had felt the first temptation in Los Angeles and Santa Monica, back when I was desperately trying to apply sunscreen on beach visitors to earn money for carpooling. The devil kept appearing on my shoulder, coaxing me: "Credit card, credit card, credit card!" But along with the devil there was also an angel who put up some resistance: "Don't do it, you twerp!" Luckily, today, the angel is more forceful, and wins the battle.

I decide not to hitchhike to Tierra del Fuego as I simply don't have any more energy for that. For this reason, I unpack my friend from my backpack; he has been hibernating there since my departure from Berlin. He is known as Ümit and is a fluffy light blue hand puppet with big eyes and a big mouth. His long-lost twin brother is known as the Cookie Monster, and appears regularly on "Sesame Street".

Ümit and I wander through Buenos Aires looking for passersby, especially tourists. I keep myself discreetly in the background while Ümit addresses the passersby politely: "Excuse me, I need to disturb you for a minute to tell you how my friend Micha and I have been traveling for more than four months around the world—without money!" Ümit cannot speak without my help, but I am a lousy ventriloquist, so I wear a fake beard. It is so long and thick and completely covers my mouth, so that any giveaway movements remain totally invisible to the passersby. There is a word for someone like me, and that word is *desesperado*. In any case, Ümit is the one being heard by the tourists, and many people first laugh and then listen as he iterates the trip. Mostly, the tourists give one peso (about 30 cents) after hearing the story of Ümit, and some even give five pesos.

The locals, though, struggle a little with Ümit, because they can't understand him properly. Some people go away without saying a word and simply leave Ümit standing there. But the majority of them are interested: *How has Ümit fared on the trip? Was it ever boring? Did he feel hungry? And is he looking forward to going back home?*

Mainly they want to know more about his twin brother, the Cookie Monster. Ümit can help them with that. He tells them how they were often confused as kids, and how they tried to look different visually. "Sesame Street" then discovered his twin brother, who became world famous, travels a lot, and is known everywhere. *But is he also happy?* Ümit tells a French couple at the Plaza de San Telmo how his brother is often drunk, and brings women home who are always after his money and his fame. The Cookie Monster had also once become addicted to gambling, and had needed to go to a psychotherapist for help.

The French couple does not understand all the details, but can hardly stop their laughter. Financially, the story of our journey catches on better with the locals, while the story of drugs, drinking and action catches on better with the Americans. A group of students from Ohio cannot get enough of the scandalous life of the Cookie Monster. They keep on asking: "Did the Cookie Monster think about suicide? Was he depressed? How many girls did he sleep with? Did you ever meet his famous friends from the show?" Ümit doesn't think much about discretion and thus tells all the private stories of the Cookie Monster, while I stand behind him with the caped beard and look towards the ground. The students from Ohio give Ümit a total of 50 pesos as thanks for the indiscreet, rather scandalous details about his famous twin brother.

On the fifth day of my stay in Buenos Aires, the soccer team, La Boca, is playing against Chacarita. It's a home game for La Boca. The passion for this team here in Argentina is like that for the Real Madrid in Spain. Diego Maradona has even played here once.

Even though I show up early at the stadium, the queue is already curving around the corner. It amazes me that a stadium this size can be sold out on a Thursday afternoon, but it's probably the norm here in Argentina. Ümit and I reach the ticket checker at the entrance and tell him that we have no money but would like to go inside. The ticket checker looks around several times thinking he must be on some candid camera show, or that this must be a joke. However, given that he is somewhat disappointed that he won't be on TV, he still lets us in. I actually can't believe that I'm going to watch the La Boca play, and for free!

The atmosphere in the stadium is overwhelming. Before the game, the fans of both teams take trash talking to a whole new level; there are a lot of references to mothers. This trash talking is interrupted again and again by loud advertisements from the loudspeakers. As soon as the ads take a break, the opposite rows continue with their screaming: *"Tu madre es una perra, una puta!"* La Boca wins three to zero. The crowd roars and loud cheers break out all around; there are people dancing, jumping and hugging each other. Gustavo, a man sitting next to me, leaps up. I had a brief conversation with him earlier about Ümit, because he found it strange that someone would bring a puppet to a football match, particularly if that someone is a full-grown, seemingly functional man. Gustavo tells me that money to him is only a means for him to see his favorite football team, La Boca. He pays 1,000 pesos for the season tickets; but even if it costs 5,000 pesos, he says that he would still pay.

With the 70 dollars I earned with Ümit, I buy a bus ticket. The distance to Ushuaia is just 2,000 miles; the remaining money should suffice until then. I only have four days before the ship departs, but I want to visit Patagonia and Tierra del Fuego. I decide to take the risk: I will take a bus to El Calafate, which covers about 1,500 miles, and from then on I will hitchhike through Patagonia and Tierra del Fuego.

The next 30 hours on the bus basically consist of me sitting and sleeping. The food is included in the price of the ticket, which I hadn't expected. We eventually reach El

Calafate, a small mountain town which has been beautifully restored. It's the closest town to the Perito Moreno Glacier, making it one of Patagonia's favorite tourist destinations.

From here I need to hitchhike further. While just three days ago in Buenos Aires the weather was hot and humid at about 90 degrees Fahrenheit, here it is just 41 degrees Fahrenheit. El Calafate lies in the middle of the Andes Mountains so even in the spring (beginning of November) it is bitingly cold. Majestic snow-covered mountains, large brown fields, and beautiful blue lakes surround me, but at the moment I couldn't care less about the scenery. My hands are freezing from holding up my cardboard sign in this temperature, so I hang the sign around my neck and put my hands in my pockets. The sun is shining and in theory the warmth from the sun is welcomed, but because I'm high up in the alpine countryside, due to the thinning ozone layer, UV rays are a concern. For this reason, almost every tourist guide warns you not to stay in the sun for too long. Unfortunately, I don't have a choice; I have to find a ride.

A bus driver sees my sign and stops. He takes me along on the six-hour trip to Rio Grande in Tierra del Fuego. The bus is brand new and is being transferred to a hotel in the city. So not only am I the only passenger on the bus, but the very first one as well. Upon arriving in Rio Grande, the first thing to do is look for an inexpensive hostel with the last of Ümit's earnings, which I find. The temperature is freezing outside. Despite my exhaustion, however, I can hardly sleep. The whole night, I keep thinking that if I am able to cover the last leg tomorrow to Ushuaia, which is just 135 miles away, I will be at the harbor two days before expected and will certainly be able to catch the ship.

Quite fatigued but full of adrenaline, I get up the next morning and start early with my sign to Ushuaia. Two hours pass before Marcello stops in his pick-up truck. He says the magic word: "USHUAIA!!" We travel past fields of fresh snow, quiet lakes nestled between mountains, and fir trees along the road. Marcello comes from Mendoza, a city in northwestern Argentina known for its vineyards and pleasant climate. Still, he ended up here in freezing Tierra del Fuego, about 1,800 miles south of his hometown, for work and higher salary. Tourism is partly the reason why there is more work in this city, but mostly it's due to the large tax benefits the government offers in order to attract more companies. Tierra del Fuego is also Argentina's center for electronic products.

Marcello has recently turned 40 years old and is financially doing well for himself. Although he misses his relatives and friends in Mendoza, he knows that he would never earn as much there as he would here. However, there are always sacrifices. "There may be money here, but not many single women," he informs me, somewhat grimly.

It's the 7th of November and I finally arrive in Ushuaia. I can hardly contain my happiness. Marcello is left in wonder when I get out of his truck, and calls out behind me, "Say hi to the ladies in the strip clubs for me!" At this moment, though, naked ladies are the last thing on my mind. Ushuaia has a population of 60,000, and winters here are extremely cold with temperatures down to -4 degrees Fahrenheit; even during the summertime, it only manages to get up to 59 degrees. I see a lot of tourists in Ushuaia who are probably stuck on the idea of seeing the southernmost city in the world. On most of the street corners, what with Antarctica less than 700 miles away, I see many promotional signs reading: *Fin del Mundo*. That is, of course, "The End of the World."

After some time I come to the office of *Antarctic Dream*. In the office, Sabina, the employee with whom I have been exchanging e-mails, welcomes me. I can tell that she is surprised that I have actually made it here. She takes me to a company-owned holiday apartment where I can stay for the next two days. With still one day left before the departure, I make use of my time by visiting one of the highlight attractions.

Near Ushuaia is a tourist train with the name *El tren del fin del mundo!* (Train to the end of the world!*)* It's an old steam engine pulling three wagons through the beautiful landscape of Tierra del Fuego. The price of a ticket is 20 dollars; since I don't have this, I decide to sneak on board. An elderly couple sees me cowering below a seat hiding from the ticket agent. They smile and I know that they won't blow my cover. After ten minutes, I am given the all-clear signal: tickets will no longer be checked on the train. I sit up and enjoy the beautiful journey through the national park. While looking out of the window, it becomes clear to me how very near I am to the end of the world.

16/ The End of the World (Antarctica)

No money, but still quite elegant: penguins in Antarctica

It is four in the afternoon on the 7th of November; the very last leg of my trip has started. The intensity, uniqueness and beauty of it outshine the past 140 days as I head towards Antarctica.

The first explorer to cross the Antarctic Circle was James Cook in the year 1773. Cook apparently was in a hurry to reach Hawaii, so he didn't set foot on the continent. Not until December 14, 1911 did the Norwegian Roald Gravning Amundsen become the first man to reach the South Pole, followed by his rival Robert Falcon Scott three weeks later, who didn't survive his journey home. The fact that the first exploration took place only about 100 years ago makes it clear how special this place really is. The climate and the weather records of the continent underscore this: in August the average temperatures here are between -40 to -95 degrees Fahrenheit. Even in February, the warmest month for Antarctica, the temperature seldom exceeds 5 degrees.

Antarctica is also the windiest continent in the world. During a long-term measurement in the Commonwealth Bay, average wind speeds of 45 miles per hour have been recorded and the highest speed has been 150 miles per hour. Yet despite the snow, Antarctica is the driest of all the continents.

The *Antarctic Dream* is the ship that I will be traveling on. It was specially built in the Netherlands in 1959 for its rough trips to the South Pole. From 1959 to 2004 it served the Chilean Navy, and after that it was rebuilt for trips to Antarctica. There are 40 double cabins so that a maximum of 80 passengers can be accommodated. In addition, the ship has a crew of 25. On the roof there is a helipad, and Zodiacs, which are the rubber rafts that can be lowered into the water by means of a crane. As compared to the container ship that brought me from Europe, the *Antarctic Dream* is much smaller, with a length of just about 270 feet; it is also much lighter. This is something I come to learn in the first two days while crossing the Drake Passage, a strait between South America and Antarctica that is about 500 miles long. This passage acts as a floodgate for the winds blowing from the west.

A few hours after departing from the harbor of Ushuaia, I go to the bridge to say hello to the captain. He warns me not to go on either of the side wings of the bridge, because they are not protected against the wind. Naturally, I want to test this out immediately: the distance is hardly 16 yards from the rear part of the right wing of the bridge to the front part. How much time do I need to reach the front? I battle through the wind at every step, mostly with one hand on the railing, in order not to be blown into the water. I take a few more steps before I slip and fall onto the ground. From here, I crawl on all fours until the target: 20 seconds for 16 yards. The forces of nature definitely have an upper hand here.

The next morning I wake up in my cabin feeling very ill. My stomach is aching intensely. The ship is swaying by about 20 degrees from left to right. Just for comparison:

steep mountain passes in the Alps often have straight ascents of 10 to 15 percent. 20 percent swaying from left to right and then from right to left, all in half a minute, are simply brutal. I try to concentrate on other things in order to divert my attention from the pain. That doesn't help, so I search for the doctor on the ship. He gives me two tablets to take for seasickness. Only five minutes after I take the first tablet, I start to vomit; the same thing happens when I take the second tablet. After a few more encounters with the toilet, I need something else to stop it: plaster. If you place a small piece behind the ear, it will help the body not to perceive the extreme swaying of the ship. I later find out that, at least, I wasn't the only one who suffered.

Everything at dinner—the décor, four-course menus, the piano player, the friendly service—impresses me. It's hard to believe that I'll spend the last ten days of my journey being spoiled in luxury. During the days, when I am not fulfilling my duties, I am allowed to take advantage of their leisure activities. There's a fitness center and a sauna available at any time of the day, and a library with books and DVDs. In addition, there are presentations held twice daily, talking about both the history and present-day circumstances of Antarctica.

In the beginning, I find it difficult to make use of these offers without feeling guilty, just like not filling up my plate to the fullest during a buffet. One would think that after so many months of little to no food that I would stuff my face given the opportunity like this, but this isn't the case whatsoever. During my ventures through the many shops, cafés and restaurants, each apple, bun, or even cup of water that I received gave me a feeling of success. The process was strenuous and sometimes frustrating, but in the end, always exciting.

The age of the passengers at my table range between 25 to 50 years old. They are from England, Canada, USA, France and China, mainly backpackers traveling across the world and wanting to see more than the stamped-out paths. Blake from the U.S. tells me that the main reason he set out for Antarctica is because it is, without a doubt, the least-visited continent on earth. A total of about 30,000 people visit it every year. Antarctica also has only 3,000 permanent residents, mostly scientists, who live on one of the research stations.

Petra, from Switzerland, booked this cruise because she wanted to see the huge ice masses of Antarctica before they disappear due to climate change. The Antarctic Peninsula, a huge headland, which points from Antarctica in the direction of the Drake Passage, is affected by this change even today. The leader of the expedition, Paulo, tells me that the *Antarctic Dream* now opens its season two weeks earlier than, say, five years ago, and passengers pay 4,000 to 5,000 dollars for a double room per person for the ten-day trip. During peak season, one could pay up to 15,000 dollars for a single room. Luckily for me, there is an odd number of workers on board, so I get my very own single room.

The temperatures on the Antarctic Peninsula have increased by three degrees since 1950. The Larsen Ice Shelf lying on the east coast has already lost large parts of its area since the beginning of the 20th century. Despite this, the icebergs in Antarctica are still very big: in some places the ice is about 1,600 feet thick. Some tower even higher than the highest mountain in Europe. In all, only 0.4 percent of the continent is free of ice. This extreme data does not come as a surprise, with the record temperature of -128 degrees Fahrenheit being measured at the Vostok station.

On the second day, Paulo comes to me and inquires if I have ever had any experience as a waiter. I am speechless. Waiters have the hardest job on a ship because even with the aggressive swaying, they must perform as professionally as possible. I fear that I will embarrass the company if the passengers see me staggering through the dining hall and spilling things all over the place, so we decide to test it out: I fill two cups with coffee, which I must carry on a large black tray while walking from one end of the dining hall to the other. The cups slip away from my tray and the disruption startles some passengers. Paulo then agrees that I shouldn't have any direct contact with the customers, both for the sake of the customers and the ship's reputation.

I then spend days two and three in the basement of the ship with Rodrigo, arranging the rubber boots and polar jackets according to sizes so that all passengers can be properly equipped upon reaching the shore.

Unfortunately, there ends up being a lot of confusion when distributing the boots and the jackets, as some people get two left boots, or one boot in a size 43 and the other in a size 37.

On day 4 we finally cross the Drake Passage; the winds have died down, and we land at the South Shetland Islands. These islands come before the Antarctic Peninsula and, like the rest of Antarctica, there is no noteworthy vegetation; only penguins and seals are found here. I stand at the exit of the ship and ask every passenger who wants to go ashore in the rubber dinghy to first disinfect and wash off their boots in the tank of liquid. This is to eliminate the risk of passing bacteria from the other parts of the world to the animals here, which can be very harmful.

Soon we are standing in the middle of hundreds, or perhaps even thousands of penguins; they run around us tolerantly. Since they have never had any bad experience with humans, they don't consider us as a threat. Directly near the penguin colony are beaches where numerous seals are lying around lazily, and who, like the penguins, are not at all bothered by us. Just beyond the colonies of penguins and seals appear incredible snow and ice-capped mountains.

Unfortunately for me, this excursion becomes extremely painful. I am the only passenger on the ship without special polar-proof pants, instead wearing only jeans. Within twenty minutes my legs are ice-cold and my jeans are frozen stiff. Paulo hands me a bunch of small red flags on long sticks to set up around the colony of the penguins in order to show the tourists that they should not walk directly through the colony. He looks at my jeans and becomes annoyed: "How can you go to Antarctica without polar-proof pants?" I explain to him that I have traveled without money through eleven countries and simply didn't have any means of buying them. Paulo shakes his head in disapproval.

Deception Island (or, The Island of Deceptions) will be our next offshore venture. It consists of an active volcano, which can heat up the water flowing to the sea to such an extent that one can swim in it. Unluckily, our ship sails straight into a body of thick ice. There is the sound of ice crackling, the engine ramping, and loud squeaking, until suddenly everything comes to a standstill. The *Antarctic Dream* remains stuck in ice that is 19 inches thick; they try moving it forward, backward, left, and right but nothing works. The engines are ramping at full blast in effort to move the ship, but the force of nature is just simply stronger. Finally, the overhead speakers announce that the scheduled visit to the hot springs is cancelled.

This puts a damper on things because it means that my long-awaited first step on the continent will be postponed. I look out of the porthole of my cabin and see seals lying on the packed ice about 100 feet away. They seem indifferent towards this new object stuck in their natural environment.

On the fifth day, we finally reach the Antarctic Peninsula. Huge glaciers 70 to 100 feet thick hang down from the steep slopes of the coast. This spectacular view can be seen nowhere else. Huge icebergs float in the water near the coast, which we bypass at a snail's pace. We travel through the Lemaire Channel, which is just less than 300 feet wide, and which is covered by mountains on both sides. My anticipation to finally set foot on Antarctica—especially after all that has happened in the last five months—creates a feeling of extreme ecstasy…that is, until I see Paulo, who tells me that today we'll go with the Zodiac boats through the icebergs, but we won't go on land. Still, the day remains unforgettable as we travel in rubber dinghies between 70 feet high icebergs.

Meanwhile, I notice that the need for my help is becoming less and less urgent. Despite being available for all-around work, I am probably called on for only four hours a day. For more demanding work, like lowering down the rubber rafts, Paulo tells me to stay away. He explains to me that he doesn't want to be held responsible if an unskilled worker wearing jeans falls in the water, and only sends for me for smaller legwork, like refueling the rubber rafts or scrubbing the deck.

It's the 13th of November and the sixth day of the tour: it's finally time to go offshore! Paulo gives me his spare polar-proof pants so that this day isn't remembered for any frostbite I will get—the temperatures are anywhere between -15 to 5 degrees Fahrenheit. The expedition gets postponed a little longer because Guillermo and Willi, two adventurers from Chile, have to be dropped off. Their plan is to travel through Antarctica for the next three to four months with a kayak and 770 pounds of luggage. A large part of the luggage consists of dehydrated food (also called "micro food").

Finally, it is the be-all and end-all moment. I help the passengers squeeze into their life vests, disinfect their boots, and help the elderly ones onto the rubber dinghy. When we are just about 100 yards away, the mixed feeling of excitement, anxiety and happiness can hardly be contained. Memories from the last five months flash through my mind; I can't believe I have really made it to Antarctica without a single cent from my own pocket.

The anchor is dropping; once they give the okay to unload, I leap from the side of the rubber boat, and I take my first step onto the continent of Antarctica.

I run about ecstatically through the knee-deep powder snow. Paulo calls behind me, asking whether I have gone totally crazy, but it doesn't bother me: I have made it! Towering all around me are mountains draped in deep snow and glaciers. Huge icebergs with a diameter of 20 to 50 yards are floating in the freezing water. The sun is shining so the reflection off the white landscape is almost blinding. The strong polar wind stirs up the powder snow. The thought that I am actually standing at the end of the world plays over and over in my mind! Finally, I have reached my destination. I throw myself in the deep snow and let out a big cry for probably the most intense five months of my life. I look up at the blue sky and reflect back.

Countries visited: Germany, Belgium, Canada, USA, Costa Rica, Panama, Colombia, Peru, Bolivia, Chile and Argentina.

Continents: Europe, North America, South America and Antarctica.

Temporary jobs: A butler for Harold in Cologne and for the German ambassador in Panama; an all-around first mate on the container ship to Canada; an advertising film producer in Las Vegas; the human sofa on the streets of Las Vegas; suntan oil applier on the beach of Santa Monica; the hill helper in San Francisco; a professional pillow fighter; a moving guy in Hawaii; a chorus boy in *The Magic Flute*; an unsuccessful porter in Machu Picchu; a fruit vendor in Puno; a ventriloquist in Buenos Aires with Ümit; and assistant on the *Antarctic Dream.*

Accommodations: Over 40 people took me into their homes, through either couch surfing or friends; a barn in an Amish community in Ohio; the park in Albuquerque; motels in Las Vegas; Waikiki beach in Honolulu; a Hare Krishna temple in Berkley; overnight buses and bus stations; and the freezing heights of Machu Picchu.

Food: Asked for food in over 500 shops, restaur and cafés. My most memorable meal was the steak

Nobel restaurant in Honolulu. And I won't forget the flowers on Big Island.

Transportation: A container ship; seven aircraft; a horse-drawn carriage; a bicycle; trekking; trains; hitchhiking rides in over twenty cars, trucks and buses; and the *Antarctic Dream*.

Climates: Polar, desert, subtropics, tropics, alpine, and temperate.

Final Total: 25,000 miles in 150 days.

Most importantly, I want to thank the hundreds of people who have made this impossible trip possible: Harold for hiring me as his butler; my fellow crewmates on the container ship for helping me realize what I have; the Amish community who took me in when I was most in need; Joseph in Albuquerque for teaching me some street smarts; David in Las Vegas for the nice comfort of a hotel room; Murph's dad for the flight ticket to Hawaii; Brandon for showing me how to live off the land and introducing ` to tasty flowers; Dr. Luck for introducing me to bicep ʼnts; Michael Grau for the lovely party at the ʼcia Alemana; the generous family in Cartagena m I learned that sometimes one needs just five ` twenty seconds to get a free accommodation; ʼhu porters for carrying some of my weight ʼe behind; Hedwig and Cicki for the tour and the ticket to Bolivia; the bus ʼ the free ticket that crucially helped keep the journey going; everybody on the *Antarctic Dream* for bringing this trip to such a successful end; and to all of the salespeople and waiters who made it easy for me to get enough food. THANK YOU!

Now that I'm standing here in freezing temperatures remembering what all that got me here, I have to ask myself: what did I plan to do once I got to Antarctica? During my trip, I have often wondered how I would feel or how I would react once I got here. Jump for joy, do my happy dance, run around like I'm crazy? Well, I've done all that, so now what? I could swim with the penguins, but since I didn't even bring polar-proof pants, I don't think my swimming trunks will do.

Well, I know one thing is for sure: I need to start moving around before my foot freezes. The tear in my right rubber boot is letting the cold in. But I am too late: my foot is completely numb, so Paulo helps me back to the rubber dinghy. As we sail away, I never imagined my much-awaited landing on shore would be like this. "So long, fucking Antarctica!" escapes loudly from my mouth. Paulo, aghast, questions me in English about whether I have a screw loose: first I leap off the dinghy with inexplicable cheer, and now, here I am cursing the continent.

Back on the ship, my foot finally thaws so that I c make peace with Antarctica again. This also means th can now look forward to returning to Germany: my j are almost in shreds; the crown of my tooth has falle and urgently needs replacing; my thick beard needs a good shave; my diet in the last 150 days consisted mainly of fast food, little vitamins, low fiber and high sugar. I am looking forward to get my life back in order.

What I am taking away with me through this experience? In life it's not always about more; more is more than enough. Personal happiness depends only to some extent on consumption. Despite having to carry on with no razor, torn jeans, a toothache, no food and total exhaustion, I didn't ever really feel unhappy. All the conveniences and amenities I have back home I didn't miss. The Amish community, the Filipinos on the container ship, and the family in Cartagena taught me that having less doesn't mean you have to be less happy. Rather, the lesson appears to be that it is better to give than take. Not everything in life needs to be a deal; one should give instead of investing. This is a lesson I need to keep in mind. When you really give without seeing a benefit in it or expecting a return, you open up, learn new things, and become unbelievably richer.

In retrospect, I would encourage all travel enthusiasts ...vel to the remotest corners of the earth, even in an ...ntional way, like I have done. One thing is for ... though I said it earlier, it bears repeating: the ...ge of humanity, shown to us by the media, is ...ent with reality. Naturally there are such ...ch people. But with a certain caution, ...an nature and curiosity for people and cultures, you can meet people from whom you can learn a lot.

On many occasions, I've have been carried forward by people as if riding on a wave. I have experienced different reactions towards travelers—especially those with no money—from various cultures. In North America, my individual approach was very forward in most of the encounters. People seem to appreciate creativity, innovative ideas and goals, even if it may seem unattainable at the moment. Most likely the history of North America has contributed to this attitude: European settlers who tried their luck in the New World were entirely on their own. For this reason, going from rags to riches is the American dream. Although I haven't made any actual riches, traveling to the end of the world certainly comes very close.

Everything was a little different in Latin America. I wasn't able to explain my idea of the trip to the people as well as I had in North America. Then again, my bad Spanish didn't help. However, despite being a blatant foreigner, people helped me just the same. They consider giving a natural part of their lives, because many of them know how it feels not to have anything…just like the family in Cartagena who had taken me in for five days, and the lady working for the bus company in Panama who gave me a free ticket.

The warmth and support I have received in all of these countries has been simply overwhelming.

Destination reached: what now??

To find out more about the trip, visit:
www.howtotraveltheworldforfree.com

And to find out more about Michael Wigge, visit:
www.michaelwigge.com

www.howtotraveltheworldforfree.com

CPSIA information can be obtained at www.ICGtesting.com
Printed in the USA
LVOW041529130712

289991LV00001B/36/P